SCIENTIFIC AMERICAN EXPLORES BIG IDEAS

The Science of Habits

HOW TO MAKE THEM OR BREAK THEM

The Editors of *Scientific American*

SCIENTIFIC AMERICAN EDUCATIONAL PUBLISHING

New York

Published in 2024 by Scientific American Educational Publishing
in association with **The Rosen Publishing Group**
2544 Clinton Street, Buffalo NY 14224

Contains material from Scientific American®, a division of Springer Nature America, Inc., reprinted by permission, as well as original material from The Rosen Publishing Group®.

First Edition

Scientific American
Lisa Pallatroni: Project Editor

Rosen Publishing
Danielle Haynes: Compiling Editor
Michael Moy: Senior Graphic Designer

Cataloging-in-Publication Data
Names: Scientific American Educational Publishing, editor.
Title: The science of habits : how to make them or break them / the editors of Scientific American.
Description: First edition. | Buffalo, NY : Scientific American Educational Publishing, 2024. | Series: Scientific American explores big ideas | Includes bibliographical references and index. | Audience: Grades 10-12
Identifiers: LCCN 2023034922 | ISBN 9781725350229 (library binding) | ISBN 9781725350212 (paperback)| ISBN 9781725350236 (ebook)
Subjects: LCSH: Habit–Juvenile literature.
Classification: LCC BF335 .S355 2024 | DDC 155.2/4–dc23/eng/20230802
LC record available at https://lccn.loc.gov/2023034922

Manufactured in the United States of America
Websites listed were live at the time of publication.

Cover: Wirestock Creators/Shutterstock.com

CPSIA Compliance Information: Batch # CWSA24.
For Further Information contact Rosen Publishing at 1-800-237-9932.

CONTENTS

INTRODUCTION

Have you ever woken up in the morning and gotten dressed and ready for school only to realize it's actually Saturday? Or do you struggle to stop biting your nails when you're nervous? These are examples of habits, behaviors you do regularly, sometimes without even thinking about it.

Some habits are good—they help you complete tasks and be more productive. The habit of getting ready for school ideally saves you time and ensures you don't forget important tasks you need to do each day, such as brushing your teeth, eating breakfast, and gathering your book bag. Other habits aren't so great, and we try to break them. Biting your nails can cause injury to your nail bed and possibly even an infection.

The articles in this book will explain the science behind how the brain forms and relies on routine to make humans productive and give them self-esteem. Section 1, "Making and Tracking Habits," explains how habits form and the benefit—or not—of tracking them. Section 2, "Setting Goals for a Better You," looks at how you can develop new habits to improve your life and the best way to stick to those goals. For many of us, this desire for self-improvement coincides with the making of New Year resolutions. In Section 3, "The Meeting of Procrastination and Motivation," writers explore how to stop procrastinating and instead motivate yourself to create new habits and accomplish tasks. Section 4, "Self-Discipline," explores the all-too-common enemy of changing habits—a lack of willpower or ability to stick to new routines. Finally, Section 5, "The Habits of Addiction and Compulsion," explores how habits can be a key symptom of certain illnesses, physical and mental. The uncontrolled repetition of small, daily habits or rituals could be a sign of obsessive-compulsive disorder, for example.

Section 1: Making and Tracking Habits

How the Brain Makes and Breaks Habits

By Anne M. Graybiel and Kyle S. Smith

Every day we all engage in a surprising number of habitual behaviors. Many of them, from brushing our teeth to driving a familiar route, simply allow us to do certain things on autopilot so that our brains are not overtaxed by concentrating on each brushstroke and countless tiny adjustments of the steering wheel. Other habits, such as jogging, may help keep us healthy. Regularly popping treats from the candy dish may not. And habits that wander into the territory of compulsions or addictions, such as overeating or smoking, can threaten our existence.

Even though habits are a big part of our lives, scientists have had a hard time pinning down how the brain converts a new behavior into a routine. Without that knowledge, specialists have had difficulty helping people break bad habits, whether with medicines or other therapies.

New techniques are finally allowing neuroscientists to decipher the neural mechanisms that underlie our rituals, including defining our so-called habit circuits—the brain regions and connections responsible for creating and maintaining our routines. The insights from this work are helping neuroscientists to figure out how the brain builds good habits and why all of us seem to struggle with breaking habits that we do not particularly care for, as well as those we are told to stop by doctors or loved ones. The research suggests that by deliberately conditioning our brain, we might be able to control habits, good and bad. That promise springs from one of several surprises: that even when it seems we are acting automatically, part of our brain is dutifully monitoring our behavior.

What Is a Habit, Really?

Habits seem to stand out as clear-cut actions, but neurologically, they fall along a continuum of human behavior.

At one end of that continuum are behaviors that can be done automatically enough to let us free up brain space for different pursuits. Others can command a lot of our time and energy. Our habits emerge naturally as we explore our physical and social environments and our inner feelings. We try out behaviors in particular contexts, find which ones seem beneficial and not too costly, and then commit to those, forming our routines.

We all begin this process when we are very young. Yet it comes with a trade-off that can work against us. The more routine a behavior becomes, the less we are aware of it. We lose the fully alert surveillance of that behavior. Did I actually turn off the stove before I left the house? Did I lock the door? This loss of surveillance not only can interfere with our daily functioning, it also can allow bad habits to creep up on us. Many people who gain weight, just a couple of pounds at a time, suddenly realize that they have been going to the snack aisle or the doughnut shop more and more frequently, scarcely thinking about it as they do.

This insidious failure to check our actions also means that habits can become akin to addictions. Witness computer gaming, Internet gambling, and constant texting and tweeting—and of course alcohol and drug use. A repetitive, addiction-driven pattern of behavior can take over part of what had been deliberate choice. Neuroscientists are still grappling with whether addictions are like normal habits, only more so, although they certainly can be thought of as extreme examples at the other end of the continuum. So can certain neuropsychiatric conditions such as obsessive-compulsive disorder—in which thoughts or actions become all-consuming—and some forms of depression, in which negative thoughts may run in a continuous loop. And extreme forms of habit may be involved in autism and schizophrenia, in which repetitive, overly focused behaviors are a problem.

Deliberate Behavior Becomes Routine

Although habits fall along different parts of the behavior spectrum, they share certain core features. Once they form, for example, they are stubborn. Tell yourself to "stop doing that," and most of the time the lecture fails! Part of the reason may be that this critique usually happens too late, after the behavior plays out and its consequences are being felt.

This stubbornness, in particular, has been a clue to uncovering the brain circuitry responsible for habit formation and maintenance. Habits become so ingrained that we perform them even when we do not want to, in part because of what are called "reinforcement contingencies." Say you do A, and then you are rewarded somehow. But if you do B, then you are not rewarded or are even punished. These consequences of our actions–the contingencies–push our future behavior one way or another.

Signals discovered in the brain seem to correspond to this reinforcement-related learning, as shown in studies originally conducted by Wolfram Schultz and Ranulfo Romo, both then at the University of Fribourg in Switzerland, and today modeled by computational scientists. Particularly important are "reward-prediction error signals," which, after the fact, indicate the mind's assessment of how accurate a prediction about a future reinforcement actually turned out to be. Somehow the brain computes these evaluations, which sculpt our expectations and add or subtract value from particular courses of action. By monitoring our actions internally and adding a positive or negative weight to them, the brain reinforces specific behaviors, shifting actions from deliberate to habitual–even when we know we should not gamble or overeat.

We and others wondered what goes on in the brain's wiring to cause this shift and whether we could interrupt it. In the Graybiel lab at the Massachusetts Institute of Technology, our group began experiments to decipher which brain pathways were involved and how their activity might change as habits formed.

First, we needed an experimental test for determining whether a behavior is a habit. British psychologist Anthony Dickinson had devised one in the 1980s that is still widely used. He and his colleagues taught lab rats in a test box to press a lever to receive a food treat as a reward.

When the animals had learned this task well and were back in their cages, the experimenters "devalued" the reward, either by letting the rats eat the reward to the point of oversatiation or by giving them a drug that produced mild nausea after the reward was eaten. Later on, they brought the rats back to the experimental box and gave them the choice of pressing the lever or not. If a rat pressed the lever even though the reward was now sickening, Dickinson considered the behavior to be a habit. But if a rat was "mindful"–if we can speak of mindfulness in a rat–then it did not press the lever, as though it realized that the reward was now unpleasant; it had not formed a habit. The test gave scientists a way to monitor whether or not a shift from purposeful to habitual behavior had occurred.

Imprinting a Habit on the Brain

By using variations of this basic test, researchers, including Bernard Balleine of the University of Sydney and Simon Killcross of the University of New South Wales in Australia, have found clues suggesting that different brain circuits take the lead as deliberate actions become habitual. New evidence from experiments on rats, as well as on humans and monkeys, now points to multiple circuits that interconnect the neocortex–regarded as the crowning glory of our mammalian brain–and the striatum, at the center of the more primitive basal ganglia, which sit at the core of our brain. These circuits become more or less engaged as we act deliberately or habitually.

We taught rats and mice to perform simple behaviors. In one task, they learned to run down a T-shaped maze once they heard a click. Depending on an audio "instruction" cue that then sounded as they ran, they would turn left or right toward the top of the T and run to that end to receive one kind of reward or another. Our goal was to understand how the brain judges the pros and cons of behaving in a particular way and then stamps a sequence of behavior as a "keeper"–a habit. Our rats certainly did develop habits! Even when a reward had become distasteful, the rats would run to it when the instruction tone sounded.

To figure out how the brain stamps a behavior as one to make a habit, the M.I.T. lab began recording the electrical activity of small collections of neurons (brain cells) in the striatum. What our group found surprised us. When the rats were first learning the maze, neurons in the motor-control part of the striatum were active the whole time the rats were running. But as their behavior became more habitual, neuronal activity began to pile up at the beginning and end of the runs and quieted down during most of the time in between. It was as though the entire behavior had become packaged, with the striatal cells noting the beginning and end of each run. This was an unusual pattern; what seemed to be happening was that the striatal cells were malleable and could help package movements together while leaving relatively few "expert cells" to handle the details of the behavior.

This pattern reminded us of the way the brain lays down memories. We all know how helpful it is to remember a string of numbers as larger units instead of one by one–such as thinking of a phone number as "555-1212" instead of "5-5-5-1-2-1-2." The late American psychologist George A. Miller coined the term "chunking" to refer to this packaging of items into a memory unit. The neural activity we observed at the beginning and end of a run seemed similar. It is as though the striatum sets up boundary markers for chunks of behavior–habits–that the internal evaluation process has decided should be stored. If true, this maneuver would mean that the striatum essentially helps us combine a sequence of actions into a single unit. You see the candy dish, and you automatically reach for it, take a treat and eat it "without thinking."

Researchers have also identified a "deliberation circuit," which involves another part of the striatum and is active when choices are not made on autopilot and instead require some decision making.

To understand the interplay between these deliberation and habit circuits, our group's Catherine Thorn recorded signals in both circuits simultaneously. As the animals learned a task, activity in the deliberation part of the striatum became strong during the middle of the runs, especially when the rats had to decide which way to turn at the top of the T, based on the instruction tone. This pattern was almost the exact opposite of the chunking pattern that we had seen in the habit striatum. And yet the activity did recede as the behavior became fully habitual. The pattern means that as we learn habits—at least as rats do—habit-related circuits gain strength, but changes in related circuits occur, too.

Because the striatum works together with a habit-related part of the neocortex at the front of the brain known as the infralimbic cortex, we then recorded activity in that region. This was an eye-opener as well. Even though we saw the beginning-and-end pileup of activity in the habit striatum, during the initial learning period we saw very little change in the infralimbic cortex. It was not until the animals had been trained for a long time and the habit became fixed that the infralimbic activity changed. Strikingly, when it did, a chunking pattern then developed there, too. It was as though the infralimbic cortex was the wise one, waiting until the striatal evaluation system had fully decided that the behavior was a keeper before committing the larger brain to it.

Stop That!

We decided to test whether the infralimbic cortex has online control over whether a habit can be expressed by using a new technique called optogenetics. With this technique, we could place light-sensitive molecules in a tiny region of the brain, and then, by shining light on the region, we could turn the neurons in that region on or off. We experimented with turning off the infralimbic cortex in rats that had fully acquired the maze habit and had formed the chunking pattern. When we turned off the neocortex just for a few seconds while the rats were running, we totally blocked the habit.

The habit could be blocked rapidly, sometimes immediately, and the habit blockade endured even after the light was turned off. The rats did not stop running in the maze, however. It was just the habitual runs to the devalued reward that were gone. The animals still ran just fine to reach the good reward on the other side of the maze. In fact, as we repeated the test, the rats developed a new habit: running to the good-reward side of the maze no matter what cue they were given.

When we then inhibited the same tiny piece of infralimbic cortex, we blocked the new habit–and the old habit instantly reappeared. This return of the old habit happened in a matter of seconds and lasted for as many runs as we tested, without our having to turn off the infralimbic cortex again.

Many people know the feeling of having worked hard to break a habit only to have it come back, full-blown, after a stressful time or after one relapse. When Russian scientist Ivan Pavlov studied this phenomenon in dogs many years ago, he concluded that animals never forget deeply conditioned behaviors such as habits. The most they can do is suppress them. We are finding the same stubbornness of habits in our rats. Yet remarkably, we can toggle the habits on and off by manipulating a tiny part of the neocortex during the actual behavior. We do not know how far this control could reach. For example, if we taught the rats three different habits in a row, then blocked the third one, would the second habit appear? And if we then blocked the second one, would the first one appear?

A key question was whether we could prevent a habit from forming in the first place. We trained rats just enough to have them reach the correct end of the T but not enough for the behavior to settle in as a habit. We then continued the training, but during each run we used optogenetics to inhibit the infralimbic cortex. The rats continued running well in the maze, but they never acquired the habit, despite many days of overtraining that usually would have made the habit permanent. A group of control rats that underwent the same training without the optogenetic interruption did form the habits normally.

Breaking Bad Habits

Our experiments offer some curious lessons. First, no wonder habits can be so difficult to break–they become laid down and marked as seemingly standardized chunks of neural activity, a process involving the work of multiple brain circuits.

Yet surprisingly, even though habits seem nearly automatic, they are actually under continual control by at least one part of the neocortex, and this region has to be online for the habit to be enacted. It is as though the habits are there, ready to be reeled off, if the neocortex determines that the circumstances are right. Even if we are not conscious of monitoring our habitual behaviors–after all, that is a large part of their value to us–we have circuits that actively keep track of them on a moment-to-moment basis. We may reach out for the candy dish without "thinking," but a surveillance system in the brain is at work, like a flight-monitoring system in an airliner.

So how close are we to helping people clinically? It will likely be a long time before anyone can flip a switch to zap away our pesky habits. The experimental methods that we and others are using cannot yet be translated directly to people. But neuroscience is changing at lightning speed, and those of us in the field are closing in on something truly important: the rules that habits work by. If we can fully understand how habits are made and broken, we can better understand our idiosyncratic behaviors and how to train them.

It is also possible that our expanding knowledge could even help people at the severe end of the habit spectrum, providing clues for how to treat obsessive-compulsive disorder, Tourette's syndrome, fear or post-traumatic stress disorder.

Drug treatments and other emerging therapies could possibly do the trick to help with such harmful habits. But we are also impressed by how the lessons we have learned from this brain research support behavioral therapy strategies, which are often suggested for helping us to establish healthy habits and weed out unhealthy ones. If you want to condition yourself to jog in the morning, then perhaps you should put out the running shoes the night before, where you cannot miss them when you wake up the next day. This visual cue mimics the audio cue we used to train the rats—and it could be especially effective if you reward yourself after the jog. Do this on enough mornings, and your brain might develop the chunking pattern that you want. Alternatively, if you want to forgo the candy dish, you could remove it from the living room or office—eliminating the cue.

Changing habits might never be easy. As Mark Twain said, "Habit is habit, and not to be flung out the window by any man, but coaxed downstairs one step at a time." Our experiments, however, lead us to an optimistic point of view: by learning more about how our brains establish and maintain routines, we hope we can figure out how people can coax themselves out of undesirable habits and into the ones they want.

Referenced

Habits, Rituals, and the Evaluative Brain. Ann M. Graybiel in *Annual Review of Neuroscience*, Vol. 31, pages 359–387; July 2008.

Human and Rodent Homologies in Action Control: Corticostriatal Determinants of Goal-Directed and Habitual Action. Bernard W. Balleine and John P. O'Doherty in *Neuropsychopharmacology*, Vol. 35, pages 48–69; 2010.

Optogenetic Stimulation of Lateral Orbitofronto-Striatal Pathway Suppresses Compulsive Behaviors. Eric Burguière et al. in *Science*, Vol. 340, pages 1243–1246; June 7, 2013.

About the Authors

Ann M. Graybiel is an Institute Professor at the Massachusetts Institute of Technology and an investigator at the McGovern Institute for Brain Research at M.I.T.

Kyle S. Smith is an assistant professor of psychological and brain sciences at Dartmouth College.

Using Behavioral Science to Build an Exercise Habit

By Katherine L. Milkman and Angela Duckworth

Spring has finally sprung, which means bathing suit season is just around the corner. That ominous thought will lead many Americans to start a workout routine in the coming weeks, but having great abs at the beach isn't the most important reason to exercise. Too little exercise is responsible for 9% of premature deaths worldwide, and we know that physical activity improves mental health as well as reducing the risk of diabetes, heart disease, and cancer. In spite of that, less than half of Americans exercise as much as they should.

So what's the problem? It's the same challenge that stands in the way of attaining most goals: a combination of forgetfulness, procrastination, and limited motivation. Thankfully, the field of behavioral science has solutions to offer.

1. Make It Social

Scheduling workouts with other people has many scientifically-proven benefits. Finding a workout buddy ensures you'll be held accountable for skipping a visit. It also makes exercise more fun (assuming you pick a buddy you like), and builds on the fact that we like to do the same things we see our friends doing. The next time you want to kick-start an exercise routine, find a workout buddy to help.

2. Pick the Right Day for a Fresh Start

Our motivation to tackle new things naturally ebbs and flows. Some days feel particularly well-suited to new beginnings because they signal to us that change is in the air. These are dates like the start of a new year, a new season, or even a new week. Birthdays also boost fresh start feelings and can be a great time to initiate a new routine. Pick a date that feels like a fresh start to you, and use it to motivate the launch of a new a workout habit.

3. Set a Tough Goal with Wiggle Room

Goals are highly motivating. Research indicates that many marathon runners use goals to improve their performance. If you look at the finishing times for millions of marathon runners, they pile up before round numbers like 4 hours and 5 hours. This suggests runners aim for these round number race times and then manage their performance to ensure they finish on track. The most useful goals are tough to achieve but not impossible. Recent research suggests setting ambitious goals with some wiggle room is particularly valuable. For instance, give yourself a "free pass" if you, say, miss one or two days of exercise one week when aiming to work out daily. You can create workout goals that are ambitious, but be sure to let yourself off the hook if you occasionally fall just shy of them.

4. Keep Trying for at Least a Month

Research has shown that rewarding people with small sums of cash every time they visit the gym for a month can lead to a lasting exercise routine. Since only a month of repetition is needed to build lasting habits, be sure that when you try jumpstarting a workout routine, you keep at it intensively for at least 28 days. That should be long enough to generate lasting change.

5. Step Up

If acting on the above tips sounds hard, a team has come together to make things easier: nearly fifty of the most talented minds in economics, psychology, computer science, neuroscience and medicine, including multiple Nobel laureates, members of the

National Academies of Sciences, MacArthur "genius" award winners, best-selling authors, and TED speakers. We've built a free, non-profit, 28-day online program that only takes a few minutes of commitment each week to kick-start an exercise habit. It's called the StepUp Program and exists thanks to the University of Pennsylvania.

The program is science in action–it's packed with the best ideas about how to promote exercise from behavioral scientists, and we're testing fifty-seven different variants of these best practices to figure out what most effectively helps people establish a workout habit at 24 Hour Fitness gyms around the country. When we're done crunching the numbers on the ingredients that yield the most benefit to StepUp Program participants, we'll share our recipe for creating a lasting habits with the world.

About the Authors

Katherine L. Milkman is a professor at the Wharton School of the University of Pennsylvania who researches behavioral economics and co-directs the Behavior Change for Good Initiative, which created the StepUp Program.

Angela Duckworth is a professor of psychology at the University of Pennsylvania, the CEO of Character Lab, and the best-selling author of Grit: The Power of Passion and Perseverance. *She studies motivation and co-directs the Behavior Change for Good Initiative, which created the StepUp Program.*

Nail Biting May Arise from Perfectionism

By Susan Cosier

Many people think of nail biting as a nervous habit, but the driving force may not be anxiety. Mounting evidence shows that people who compulsively bite their nails, pick their skin or pull their hair are often perfectionists, and their actions may help soothe boredom, irritation and dissatisfaction.

As many as one in 20 people suffer from body-focused repetitive disorders, engaging in behaviors such as biting their nails or plucking out hair until they damage their appearance or cause themselves pain. These disorders are related to tic disorders and, more distantly, obsessive-compulsive disorder. As such, the repetitive behavior is extremely difficult to quit–yet many people continue to think they simply have a nervous habit and are too weak-willed to overcome it.

A new study adds evidence to a theory that perfectionism rather than anxiety is at the root of these behaviors. The researchers first surveyed 48 participants, half of whom had these disorders and half of whom did not, on their organizational behavior and ability to regulate their emotions. Those with the disorders scored as organizational perfectionists, indicating a tendency to overplan, overwork themselves and get frustrated quickly without high levels of activity.

Researchers then put the subjects in situations designed to provoke four different emotions: to incite stress, they showed a movie of a plane crash; to promote relaxation, they showed a movie of waves; to elicit frustration, they presented a difficult puzzle but said it was easy; and to evoke boredom, they made participants sit in a room alone. People who had the disorders engaged in the body-focused behaviors during all the situations except the relaxing movie.

The work, which was published earlier this year in the *Journal of Behavior Therapy and Experimental Psychiatry*, jibes with a recent theory that stress is far from the sole cause of these compulsions. Boredom and frustration, easily elicited by an underlying perfectionist personality, may be more important triggers. Past research suggests that the biting or scratching indeed makes people feel better temporarily—perhaps satisfying the perfectionist urge to be doing something rather than nothing. After the initial relief, however, comes pain, shame and embarrassment.

The findings could help therapists treat patients who suffer from the disorders; studies have shown that these types of perfectionist beliefs and behaviors can be eased with cognitive-behavior therapy. If patients can learn to think and act differently when tension builds, they may be able to stop the urge before it starts.

About the Authors

Susan Cosier is a freelance journalist focused on science and the environment. She is based in Chicago. Follow Cosier on Twitter @susancosier.

When Old Habits Die Easy

By Christie Nicholson

Some say it's tough to break a habit–a behavior so ingrained in our mental infrastructure that it's automatic. But new research says maybe it's not so tough when you shine some light on an alternative.

Turns out that a small part of the brain's prefrontal cortex–the infralimbic cortex–is key to seemingly inflexible, habitual behavior.

Scientists trained rats to run a maze by using rewards. Eventually the rats ran the maze without any reward, or even when being punished by completing it with a drink that made them nauseous. So running the maze in a certain direction had become a habit.

The scientists then used what's called optogenetics–a procedure that uses light to stimulate or inhibit specific brain areas–to turn "off" this small brain area involved in forming habits.

Within seconds the rats stopped running the maze in the direction that gave them the icky reward. The scientists note that silencing the neurons in that brain area allowed the rats to have more cognitive control over their supposedly reflexive habit of running in that one direction.

The hope is to eventually treat disorders involving obsessive or addictive behavior. And to hopefully show that old habits can die easy.

Tracking Your Steps and Other Behaviors Isn't Always the Greatest Idea

By Zeynep Tufekci

I was among the many people excited by fitness trackers and purchased one soon after they came out. It was fun. Look, 20,000 steps in one day (trip to a new city)! Two nights this week of uninterrupted sleep and 21 miles walked!

There's something captivating about numbers, which can explain the existence of the quantified-self phenomenon–that is, people who measure many things about themselves. Nowadays a smartwatch or even just your phone can keep track of a wide variety of markers, including heart rate, sleep patterns, steps in a day and even arrhythmias. People who run, swim or bike can measure their pace, distance covered, calories burned or total exercise time. A clip on your lapel can monitor your exposure to the sun. And perhaps warming the heart of every parent who got tired of reminding their children to "stand up straight," you can even wear a device that buzzes you if you slump for more than, say, 15 seconds!

You can even spice it all up with "gamification," setting up daily or weekly goals, and the program will award you badges and play celebratory tunes when you hit them. You can also upload your data to share with others–perhaps in friendly competition. Meanwhile workplace wellness programs that offer incentives or discounts on health insurance to employees who use such tracking devices and meet certain goals are spreading.

Unfortunately, despite some early encouraging studies that suggested that wearers of such devices were healthier than those who were not, the first large-scale experimental study, where people were randomly assigned to wear a fitness tracker, showed no difference in outcomes. Findings are similarly discouraging for workplace wellness programs: early research hopefully suggested that they were effective for lowering health care expenditures. But once again, better-designed studies showed practically no difference in outcomes over time.

What's going on? In fact, probably something very common. Early studies for new treatments or devices tend to be observational: they compare individuals who have chosen to take a specific action (eat a healthy diet; exercise regularly) with those who do not. Yet that engenders confounding biases because of the way people self-select into the groups, a problem that can be resolved only with true randomized experiments.

Should you sport one anyway? One concern is that these tracking devices are ... tracking devices. Many also track location, and they've already been invoked in court cases. In one, the unfortunate victim's heart rate spiked significantly and then stopped while the suspect was with her despite his claims he had left before she died. Solving a murder is good, but it's easy to imagine health insurers or employers requiring a certain number of steps a day or using such health data for making decisions.

When I first got my tracker, I tried to hit 10,000 steps a day. It felt gratifying when it catalogued 10-plus-day streaks of meeting my goals. This is called the Hawthorne effect, after experiments in a relay factory outside Chicago, Hawthorne Works, showed productivity increased when the lights were turned up–but also when the lights were turned down. A change, any change, and a feeling of being observed seem to put us on alert and better behavior–but only for a time. The novelty does wear off, and then we return to our baseline behavior.

Still, could it hurt to know the number? Maybe. Employees who were offered financial rewards along with a tracker fared worse after the trial ended and the cash dried up as compared with those who had never been offered incentives. External rewards seem to "crowd out" internal motivations–and once they go away, we don't always get the internal motivation back.

When my wrist tracker broke down after about a year, I just didn't feel like shelling out for another one. Anyway, even by the end of the third month, I could pretty reliably guess my steps or hours of sleep for the day without checking the app. Instead I took inspiration from people who argue that exercise is also about the right ecology—individuals in walkable cities get a lot more than those in suburbia, for example. So I now have a treadmill desk at work, and I set things up at home so that almost all my TV viewing is done on an elliptical. And honestly, I get cranky if I don't get some movement in during the day. That seems to be the best motivation to keep turning those pedals.

About the Author

Zeynep Tufekci is an associate professor at the University of North Carolina School of Information and Library Science and a regular contributor to the New York Times. *Her book,* Twitter and Tear Gas: The Power and Fragility of Networked Protest, *was published by Yale University Press in 2017.*

Self-Tracking Your Resolutions

By Enrique Rueda and Karla Erickson

Millions of Americans make New Year's resolutions each year, with losing weight, eating healthier and focusing on wellness among the most popular goals. Many look to self-tracking gadgets for support. But while tools like Fitbits and Apple Watches, and apps like Happier and Sleep Cycle, promise utility and convenience, they also introduce unintended consequences that may make you think twice about how to reach your goals. Self-tracking tools may help us be more fit or productive, but can also lead users to feel insecure and competitive, while providing new inroads for corporate monitoring of our daily habits.

Today's Fitbits and built-in step-trackers (in phones, watches and even shirts) have their roots at least as far back as the late 18th century, when some early pedometers were developed. Today, new tools allow users to track key facets of daily life including productivity, fitness, sleep and even more minute details such as cups of water consumed. On the surface, these seem like harmless metrics for improvements in health and well-being.

Yet quantifying activities in daily life becomes ground not only for discussion but also for comparison and sometimes even competition. Self-tracking devices provide a kind of social currency: if you've taken more steps, you're somehow a "better" person. But if you haven't reached your goal, you're a failure. As such, self-tracking can induce or reinforce negative self-image. In addition, such comparisons can distract from the act of counting and progressing along individual measures, and shift to a focus on using those measure to compete, and beat, peers. The goals become less about ourselves and more about others, which can cause people to bend the truth about what they're tracking or give up altogether.

Research shows that sharing goals with family and friends makes success at new habit development more likely. But when we track, we have committed to a view that our current bodies, lifestyles and habits are not enough. This can be stress-inducing by itself, but the act of tracking can also add one more to-do item to our ever-growing lists, introducing new pressures and a feeling that we've given control of our bodies over to an app or gadget.

Self-tracking also encourages us to turn our connection to our bodies over to a machine. Using sleep or hydration trackers encourages users to wait for the electronic nudge from our phone rather than internal signals of fatigue or thirst. Such reliance runs the risk of encouraging us to discount our body's knowledge.

Interestingly, individuals are not the only ones interested in our goals, longings and daily accomplishments and failures. Corporations gain access to the minutiae and intimate details of daily life when we enter our behaviors into self-tracking devices, acquiring our data for free–something scholars call "data exhaust." When we track, we often lose ownership over our data; every step that is tracked or calorie counted are data being mined, bought and sold by big corporations. As such, self-tracking data has a high value for corporate interests. What begins as a private health goal also brings in other interested parties, including companies that want more active employees, corporations attempting to sell to people like you, and even insurance companies interested in more real-time health information about the people they insure.

So, when it comes time to choose tactics for achieving your goals, choose wisely. Incorporate face-to-face measures as well as apps; select any tools you employ carefully, and trust the messages your body provides, not just the digital assistants that help you make and remake yourself.

The views expressed are those of the author(s) and are not necessarily those of Scientific American.

About the Authors

Enrique Rueda is a senior in sociology at Grinnell College.

Karla Erickson is a professor of sociology and feminist ethnographer of labor at Grinnell College. She is the author of The Hungry Cowboy, How We Die Now *and the forthcoming* Messy Humans: A Sociology of Machine/Human Relations.

Section 2: Setting Goals for a Better You

New Year's Resolutions are Notoriously Slippery, but Science Can Help You Keep Them

By Katy Milkman

Every January nearly half of Americans make New Year's resolutions. We resolve to eat better, exercise more, get organized, spend less money, and so on. Unfortunately, several studies suggest that most of these resolutions don't stick. But it doesn't have to be that way. If you've made a resolution this year and would like help keeping it, you're in luck: Ayelet Fishbach, one of the world's foremost researchers on the science of motivation, has written a book designed for you.

Fishbach is a social psychologist at the University of Chicago Booth School of Business and author of *Get It Done: Surprising Lessons from the Science of Motivation*. I am a professor at the Wharton School at the University of Pennsylvania and author of *How to Change: The Science of Getting From Where You Are to Where You Want to Be*. I recently interviewed Fishbach about her work on what it takes to motivate us not only to get started on goals but also to see them through all the way to the finish line. In particular, she explains how adjusting our context and circumstances–for instance, our social support and how we frame progress–can help us stay motivated to finish a large project.

[An edited transcript of the interview follows.]

Milkman: This book came out right after the start of the new year. Could you give us one tip from research on how people can better set themselves up for success with their New Year's resolutions?

Fishbach: The book is about how to motivate yourself, so I'm going to choose a strategy that captures self-motivation best: give advice to someone who is struggling with a similar issue. You might hesitate to give advice about something you haven't yet mastered, but ultimately, you will not only help them, you will also motivate yourself. A paper by psychologists Lauren Eskreis-Winkler, Angela Duckworth and I found that unemployed people who gave job-hunting advice to others were more motivated to look for a job than another group of unemployed people who received advice from an expert. Giving advice also helped those struggling with losing weight, saving money and controlling their temper.

When you give advice, you recall your past successful behaviors and form specific plans of action for the future. As a result, you become more confident and committed to your success.

Milkman: You advocate putting a number on goals. Can you explain what you mean by that and why it is important?

Fishbach: I think of goals like baking recipes. You need to list the exact quantities: "walk 10,000 steps a day" is better than "walk a lot" because it tells you how much (10,000 steps) and how soon (by the end of the day). In fact, as I discuss in my book, that specific goal, which came out of a marketing effort and not health research, is so powerful because 10,000 is a memorable and exact quantity.

Targets make it easier to monitor progress. You'll know when you're halfway through or almost there. Targets also pull you toward them. If you set your target at saving $10,000 this year, you'll be disappointed if you "only" save $9,900.

A study led by Eric Allen at the University of California, Riverside, analyzed data from about 10 million marathon runners for whom a popular target time is four hours. The team found that far more people finish in three hours and 59 minutes rather than four hours and one minute. Having a good chance of beating the target time, runners push harder and run faster.

Milkman: I am really fascinated by what you call "the middle problem." Could you describe what it is and what can be done about it?

Fishbach: We're highly motivated at the beginning. Over time, our motivation declines as we lose steam. To the extent that our goal has a clear end point, such as graduating with a diploma, our motivation picks up again toward the end.

In the middle, it's harder to get things done and to do them right. In a study, Rima Touré-Tillery, now at Northwestern University, and I found that people literally cut corners. We handed people a pair of scissors and asked them to cut out five identical shapes. At first, they neatly cut their shape, but by the time they got to the third shape, they started cutting through more corners. Then, toward the fifth shape, their shapes became neat again.

The trick is to think of middles differently. Katy, your "fresh start effect" is one intervention that does this. It encourages people to use temporal landmarks such as the first day in the month to "restart" a goal, so instead of being in the middle, you feel like you're at the beginning again. Alternatively, I suggest that you keep middles short: a monthly saving goal is better than an annual saving goal.

Milkman: To keep motivated, when should we focus on what we've accomplished and when should we focus on the work that lies ahead?

Fishbach: How we monitor progress matters. At the beginning of pursuing a goal, you should look back at your completed actions. Beyond the midpoint, you should look ahead at what's still missing. In a study Minjung Koo at Sungkyunkwan University in South Korea and I conducted with a restaurant in Seoul, diners who purchased a few meals were more likely to come back if they were enrolled in a reward program that emphasized how many meals they had already purchased. But diners who had already purchased many meals were more likely to come back if they were enrolled in a reward program that emphasized how close they were to winning a free meal.

Looking back at what you've done reaffirms your commitment. If you're unsure whether a goal is worthy or whether you can do it, look back at what you've achieved. Looking ahead makes you realize how far you are from your target. If you're already committed, you'll want to make more progress when you look ahead.

Milkman: How does our experience of fun or discomfort influence our motivation?

Fishbach: You and I both have done research showing that finding the fun path to a goal is a key for persistence. But why is fun so important? The reason is that humans respond more strongly to immediate outcomes. If doing something makes you feel good while you do it, you're more likely to persist than if you think it'll make you feel good at some distant point in the future.

Fun is an immediate outcome. It increases intrinsic motivation, the sense that we are doing something for its own sake. You found that people who listen to an audiobook when they exercise, exercise more. They're intrinsically motivated to engage in the exercising-plus-listening combo.

We also respond to the feeling that we're learning. In a very recent paper that is currently in press at Psychological Science, my colleagues and I found that even slight discomfort–to the extent that it's immediate–can increase motivation if it's appraised in a certain way. When students in improvisation classes sought discomfort as a sign that they were growing their abilities, they were more engaged in the learning process. We all like immediate results.

A common mistake is to envision your future self as more goal-oriented and less fun-seeking than your present self. When you think you won't care about fun, you choose the wrong job, workout or healthy meal.

Milkman: You devote a whole section of your book to social support. What kind of social support do you think is most important to achieving a goal, and how can people go about finding it?

Fishbach: When I watched the Olympic Games last summer, it didn't inspire me to exercise. But when my spouse expects me to join him in our basement for our morning workout, it motivates me to get out of bed and into my yoga pants. The best social support comes from someone who wants you to succeed.

Milkman: If readers could remember just one thing from all the research you cover in *Get It Done*, what would you want it to be and why?

Fishbach: You influence yourself by changing your circumstances and how you think of them. Often, framing the same situation in a different way can provide a substantial boost to your motivation.

About the Author

Katy Milkman is a behavioral scientist and James G. Dinan Professor of Operations, Information and Decisions at the Wharton School at the University of Pennsylvania. She is also author of the book How to Change: The Science of Getting from Where You Are to Where You Want to Be, *host of the podcast Choiceology and co-director of the Behavior Change for Good Initiative. Follow Milkman on Twitter @Katy_Milkman.*

The Best New Year's Resolution Might Be to Just Let Go of an Unfulfilled Life Goal

By Francine Russo

Since the 19th century, when motivational science had its start, scientists have focused on what makes us persist through difficulties and achieve what we want. Only recently have they zeroed in on how we can relinquish our cherished aspirations–and why we should. They term this process "goal disengagement," and New York University research psychologist Gabriele Oettingen says it has been treated as the "black sheep" of the field.

Why is that so? Western cultural bias celebrates persistence and achievement, so abandoning goals is seen as "failure," says psychologist Cathleen Kappes of the University of Hildesheim in Germany. Kappes is guest co-editor of the December 2022 issue of *Motivation and Emotion*, which is devoted entirely to advances in goal disengagement science. The issue exemplifies a swelling movement to correct this neglect.

This work mainly focuses on long-term goals central to our lives or identity: getting a degree, finding a spouse, becoming a homeowner. Some aims may be shorter-term, such as training to run a marathon, but they all require commitment, effort and sacrifice.

Endless research and everyday experience tell us that overcoming obstacles to eventually succeed is essential for our well-being. Such initiatives can be anything from a toddler falling on her butt until she learns to walk to a law school graduate finally passing the bar.

But trying and trying again is not the whole story. What the latest science shows us is the importance of abandoning ambitions when they become too costly or their feasibility plunges, or both. Given the long-running emphasis on the value of persistence, an immediate question arises: Is letting go as critical as persisting? It's hard to know. What matters most for our well-being, Kappes says, "is rather the optimal interplay between both processes."

The ability to set goals, pursue them despite setbacks and then quit them as circumstances change is adaptive and healthy. So is finding and committing to meaningful new aspirations. Some of us are much better at doing one or both of these things, and how well we do them dramatically affects our emotional and physical health.

To measure how our natural abilities to do both these things affect people's lives, psychology professor Carsten Wrosch of Concordia University in Quebec and Michael Scheier, a professor emeritus at Carnegie Mellon University, developed the Goal Adjustment Scale (GAS). It asks people how they react when forced to stop pursuing an important goal. One self-rating component declares, "I stay committed to the goal for a long time; I can't let it go." Another says, "I seek other meaningful goals."

The GAS measures both people's ability to disengage and their ability to find and commit to new objectives. Wrosch says these are complementary but differing capabilities. Letting go means withdrawing both commitment and effort–it prevents repeated failures and leads to less stress, depression and intrusive thoughts. Committing to and working toward new ambitions create a sense of purpose in life and reduce the sense of failure.

Certain personality traits are linked to these abilities. "Optimists may feel, 'My life will be good again,' which makes it easier to let go and to reengage with new goals," Wrosch says. Psychologist Lucas Keller says he and his colleagues at the University of Konstanz in Germany have found that "people who are habitual planners (if-then thinkers) sometimes have more trouble letting go but, once free, are better at finding and going after new endeavors."

Armed with a scale to measure goal-adjustment capacities, scientists have studied their impact. A 2019 meta-analysis of 31 samples overwhelmingly shows that people who are better at letting go have better functioning endocrine and immune systems, better health behaviors and fewer physical problems. Those better at pursuing new goals are healthier and function better physically under emotional distress.

In this context, two studies are particularly striking. In one conducted by Wrosch and his colleagues, two groups of parents were compared: the first group's children had cancer, and the second group's children were healthy. The parents of healthy children had generally low depression. The parents of children with cancer, however, reported high depression if they were unable to disengage or reengage. Their counterparts who were able to disengage and reengage, by contrast, had low depressive symptoms, similar to the parents of healthy children.

Another study followed 135 adults, aged 64 to 90 years, over about six years at a time of life when physical declines often make certain desired pursuits no longer possible. For those who scored high in disengagement abilities, depressive symptoms were generally low and did not worsen. Those who scored low became more depressed over time, and at the end of the multiyear period, they reached a level of depression that warranted clinical evaluation and possible intervention.

Across a variety of studies, Wrosch and his colleagues have found that the ability to disengage is related to both lower cortisol levels and better immune function. "In the context of stress and unattainable goals," he says, "goal disengagement and goal reengagement capacities can become paramount to protect well-being and health."

When we set career or relationship targets that are closely linked to our identity, it can be hard to give them up even in the face of insurmountable barriers. We've invested a lot in getting that doctorate, trying to conceive with repeated fertility treatments, selling that invention. Deciding when–or whether–to give it up is not easy. In fact, it can be a long and complicated process in which people are torn between the need to hold on and the need to let go. University of Zurich motivation psychologist Veronika Brandstätter-Morawietz and her colleagues have termed this struggle an "action crisis." Making a decision about whether to stay or go operates on three levels: behavioral (the effort you put in), cognitive (the continued evaluation of your progress and prospects) and emotional (whether you still treasure the goal).

Such crises are hardly rare. In an unpublished study of 100 high-level executives that Brandstätter-Morawietz conducted in 2017, 60 percent said they were experiencing an action crisis at the moment, and 10 percent had experienced one previously. "Of course, this data is not representative," she says, "but it gives some idea about how common action crises are."

When you literally cannot do anything about your goal but still ruminate about it–as happened to many people through job loss during the COVID pandemic–researchers found that having a higher percentage of these "frozen goals" and fixating more on them led to greater stress, depression and anxiety. Such people had stopped working toward their goals, but they had not disengaged cognitively or emotionally.

A feeling of having no control may play a role in such outcomes. Experiments by University of Zurich psychology researcher Zita Mayer and her colleagues showed that when subjects shelved one of two desirable goals with the option of returning to the shelved goal later, they experienced less regret than those who permanently gave up on one of the goals.

Cognitive strategies exist to help people get unstuck from the pursuit of a fruitless objective. Some work by helping them reappraise the feasibility and desirability of their aims. Mindfulness can do this. It works by allowing people to free themselves from defenses and judgments, opening them up to information that may be unwelcome but is critical to accurately evaluating their progress and chances of success.

The most notable goal-focused strategy is called mental contrasting with implementation intentions (MCII), which can help people avoid bumping up against immovable objects in the first place. When MCII is used at the start, says University of Zurich psychologist Katharina Bernecker, "it might help people set goals that are attainable and mentally prepare for difficult situations."

MCII was the creation of New York University research psychologist Gabriele Oettingen. She has made it publicly available online as WOOP (Wish, Outcome, Obstacle, Plan). Tested in study after study, MCII has shown that it can achieve behavior change in areas as diverse as education, health and personal relationships. Mostly, Oettingen says, it's been used to help people persist, overcome obstacles and achieve their goals—when those goals are possible. "It's equally effective for actively disengaging from goals—when obstacles are perceived as insurmountable," she says.

MCII works this way: People identify their wish for a desired future—let's say becoming a medical doctor. They imagine the best possible outcome, being happy as an oncologist helping save cancer patients. Then they consider and imagine the critical obstacle—mediocre grades in science, for example. They think of ways to overcome the obstacle and make a plan. This might entail getting a science tutor and studying harder. If, despite these measures, they still do not score higher than a C in science courses, another MCII will help to possibly change their plan or course of action.

"Face these obstacles head-on," Oettingen says, summing up the strategy. "If you understand that they are insurmountable or that another goal is presently more urgent, you can save a lot of resources by saying, 'I better get out.' Then you can adjust your wish, postpone it to another time or let it go."

The effects of MCII, she explains, occur on all three levels: cognitive, emotional and behavioral. In many studies, it was shown to help people to stop planning for a likely futile goal. The strategy made them feel "cool" with the change and prevented them from investing energy and resources in that goal.

Oettingen applauds the recent scientific focus on letting go. "Scientists are learning to better understand the goal disengagement process and how to help people who are vexed by goals being blocked, stuck between going on versus letting go and drowning in ruminations," she says.

About the Author

Francine Russo is a veteran journalist specializing in social sciences and relationships. She is author of Love after 50: How to Find It, Enjoy It, and Keep It *(Simon and Schuster, 2021).*

Why We Think We Can Keep Those New Year's Resolutions

By Benjamin A. Converse and Marie Hennecke

Here we go again. Year after year, with great confidence each time, we choose all the goals we are going to start pursuing *next* year. Next year, we'll start eating healthier. Next year, we'll start going to the gym more. Next year, we won't check email right before bed. Why do we expect so much from ourselves *next* year?

To understand why next year holds so much promise, it's useful to consider why last year's resolutions went unfulfilled. Sure, on any given day, we would all love to kick off the day with a nutritious and delicious breakfast smoothie. But who has time to peel a mango or wash a blender? And, yes, it would feel fantastic to squeeze in a gym visit on the way home from work. But who wants to lug a gym bag to work? And, oh, the relaxation that would come from a totally unplugged evening! But is everything really all set for tomorrow's presentation? The problem for this year's goals is that they always seem to be constrained by the pesky realities of the moment.

For better or worse those pesky realities are less likely to come to mind when planners are considering the future. Our new research, soon to be published in the journal *Social Psychological and Personality Science*, shows that the mere prospect of turning a calendar page can be enough to make planners forget about the obstacles that constrain their aspirations. Goals look greener on the other side of the calendar.

In one of our studies, conducted on July 31st, we asked a group of prospective dieters to think about eating healthier the next day. They wrote down what came to mind and then we categorized their responses. We focused on whether each thought was about achieving their desired outcomes or the constraints that threaten those outcomes. Thoughts like "I'll have more energy," and "I want to lose weight" went in the outcomes category. Thoughts like "mangoes are hard to peel" and "I hate washing the blender" went in the constraints category.

For half of the participants, our survey only mentioned days of the week, not months, implying that tomorrow was part of *this* week. In this condition, thoughts about desirable outcomes were offset by awareness of the constraints. For every two thoughts about outcomes, participants wrote down nearly three thoughts about constraints. For the other half of participants, our survey highlighted that tomorrow is August 1st, implying that it was part of next month. In this condition, participants generated far fewer constraints. For every two thoughts about outcomes, participants wrote down only 1.2 thoughts about constraints. It was as if, by seeing the next day as part of a separate period, the dieters' concerns disappeared. They weren't denying the concerns. The concerns just weren't coming to mind in the first place. Why would that be?

Psychologists have known for some time, thanks to work led by Nira Liberman from Tel Aviv University and Yaacov Trope from New York University, that goals look different in the distant versus near future. Three months ago, when you booked your holiday travel, you probably had some abstract notions of "family togetherness," "relaxation," or "adventure." The night before you left, however, you probably had some more immediate concerns in mind. Concerns like, "How is all this stuff going to fit in the suitcase?" and "Will I be able to get an Uber driver at 4:45 AM?" People think about goals that are off in the distance more abstractly. It is only when goals get closer that people start to think about them more concretely. Our study showed that just being on the next page of the calendar can make goals seem more like they are off in the distance.

To determine whether this affected people's plans, we ran another experiment on a Tuesday toward the end of February. We asked prospective dieters to report their expectations about starting to eat healthier each upcoming day from Wednesday, February 27th, to Tuesday, March 4th. Some participants saw a calendar that focused them on calendar dates and others saw one that focused them on days of the week. Participants who focused on dates had low expectations for February 27th and 28th, but their expectations jumped substantially for March 1st and thereafter. In contrast, participants who focused on weekdays had low expectations for the first four days, Thursday through Sunday, but their expectations jumped substantially for Monday and thereafter. What counts as the next new period, the next opportunity, is all a matter of perspective.

So what is the upshot of these shifting perspectives? Is it good that there is always a new opportunity to get started? Or is it bad that there is always a new opportunity to put something off? There is probably not a simple answer. It depends on the conditions under which planners are looking into the future. We documented one of the potential dangers of these shifting perspectives in a final study that looked at how people use health memberships.

We ran the study in Switzerland, where Dr. Hennecke works. In exchange for completing a short health survey, participants gained entry into a raffle for one of ten memberships to a popular Swiss health program called eBalance. Bearing some resemblance to Weight Watchers in the U.S., eBalance is a paid service that tries to help people lose weight by providing calorie tracking, coaching, dietary advice, and other forms of support. The memberships were worth about $78 each.

After the survey, which we administered in mid-August, we asked participants to choose which starting date they would use if they won one of the memberships. Regardless of their choice, the membership ended on November 30th. For half of the participants, the choice was whether to start the program in one week or two weeks. In this scenario, about 60 percent chose to start on the first day. For the other half of participants, the timing was the same, but we pointed out the specific dates of the two starting options: August 25th or September 1st. In this scenario, only about 40 percent wanted to start on the first day. The prospect of starting in a new month was so attractive that many people sacrificed an extra week of valuable support.

Still, we can only say at this point that wasting a week of the dieting program was a "potential" danger. We do not know how the dieters fared in the long run. It is possible that those who waited for the 1st found it easier to initiate. That could be good in the long run, as long as they weren't sidetracked by the constraints that they presumably failed to see foresee.

The big research question going forward, then, is how to leverage this phenomenon to both encourage initiation while also supporting persistence. It can be hard to overcome the inertia of inaction or bad habits, but the positive expectations about "next week," "next month," or "next year" might help people to get going. Indeed, researchers have found that people do at least take the first step on these new beginnings. For example, Google searches for health information spike on Mondays and gym visits spike at the beginning of months, weeks, years, and other salient temporal landmarks. If you miss the bus this week, no problem, another one will be pulling up shortly.

The challenge, however, is helping people to persist after these initial steps. By definition, if health searches and gym visits peak after temporal landmarks, that means they are falling at other times. This is where our results may reflect some bad news. Expectations are high for new periods because people are not thinking as much about the upcoming constraints. In the long run, this could lead to trouble because people are unlikely to be successful in long-term goal pursuits if they have not adequately planned for the obstacles they will face.

As you're thinking ahead to 2017, remember that "next year" inevitably becomes "this year," and the same constraints will apply. Go ahead and take advantage of the fact that next year feels like a more auspicious time to start, but make hard-to-break commitments that accommodate your constraints. Don't just decide to eat healthier, sign up for a cooking co-op. Don't just promise to go to the gym more, sign up for a series of pre-paid classes that fit your schedule. Don't just vow not to check email in bed, get a router that blocks your Wi-Fi after a certain time.

And, if you fall off course, don't get preoccupied with 2018 quite yet. Aim for next Monday instead.

The views expressed are those of the author(s) and are not necessarily those of Scientific American.

Referenced

1. "goals look different..." Trope, Yaacov, and Nira Liberman. "Construal-level theory of psychological distance." *Psychological Review* 117.2 (2010): 440.
2. "Google searches for health information..." Ayers, John W., et al. "What's the healthiest day?: Circaseptan (weekly) rhythms in healthy considerations." *American Journal of Preventive Medicine* 47.1 (2014): 73-76.
3. "gym visits spike..." Dai, Hengchen, Katherine L. Milkman, and Jason Riis. "The fresh start effect: Temporal landmarks motivate aspirational behavior." *Management Science* 60.10 (2014): 2563-2582.
4. "if they have not adequately planned..." Gollwitzer, Peter M., et al. "Planning promotes goal striving." *Handbook of Self-Regulation: Research, Theory, and Applications* 2 (2011): 162-185.

About the Authors

Benjamin A. Converse is an assistant professor of public policy and psychology at the University of Virginia, in the Frank Batten School of Leadership and Public Policy and the Department of Psychology. His research focuses on self-regulation, social judgment, and decision making.

Marie Hennecke is a Senior Teaching and Research Associate at the University of Zurich in Switzerland. Her research focuses on self-regulation and motivation, with a particular focus on the processes that instigate goal setting and the processes that explain why some people are more successful in pursuing their goals than other people.

How Would a Psychologist Get in Shape?

By Victoria Stern

We asked experts on behavior change how they recommend approaching three of the most common New Year's resolutions. The advice can be generalized to just about any goal, so read on even if you have a more unusual challenge ahead of you.

Resolution #1: Eat Healthier

"New Year's resolutions are often too general," says Phillippa Lally, a research psychologist at University College London. She emphasizes identifying specific behaviors, deciding when to perform them and then doing so repeatedly. For instance, map out when you will eat your five servings of fruits and vegetables—one with each meal, one for your midday snack and one after dinner. At some point you will likely give into temptation, she says, but do not be deterred. Forming a new habit can take anywhere from 18 to 254 days, according to one study by Lally and her colleagues.

Resolution #2: Quit Smoking

"We can improve self-control through practice," says Mark Muraven, associate professor of psychology at the University at Albany. In fact, Muraven notes, increasing our willpower is similar to strengthening a muscle. In a recent study, he found that smokers remained abstinent longer if they exerted self-control in other areas, such as cutting back on desserts, before attempting to quit. Don't overdo it, though—willpower can get depleted if you try to exercise it too much. Focus on your primary goal. If you keep slipping up, cut back on other attempts to use self-control.

Resolution #3: Spend Less, Save More

"If you're uptight and stressed while trying to modify a behavior, you actually inhibit yourself from changing, but if you're playful and flexible, you may become more open to figuring out a way to reach your goal," says B. J. Fogg, an expert on behavior change at Stanford University. Changing your behavior should not feel like drudgery. To save money, for example, be creative about how to cut back. Find a quirky vintage shop to purchase your winter coat or experiment with new recipes that make cooking more enticing than eating out.

About the Author

Victoria Stern is a contributing editor at Scientific American Mind.

How to Stick to Your New Year Resolutions

By Susana Martinez-Conde

The first I ever heard of New Year resolutions was after I moved from Spain to the U.S. for my postdoctoral training, in 1997. In Spain, the New Year's party rituals are different too: instead of a countdown of the last ten seconds followed by a rendition of "Auld Lang Syne," we Spaniards close the year by eating twelve grapes of luck–or "uvas de la suerte"–one for each of the twelve strokes of midnight's bells. The grape-eating custom–said to have been started by grape growers in the early 20th century–is akin to blowing out the candles on your birthday cake. You formulate a wish just as midnight approaches (some people do twelve wishes, but I think that's just greedy). Then, if you perform the ritual without mistakes (you have no grapes left after the twelfth bell, and you pop the last grape in your mouth simultaneously with the twelfth bell), your wish(es) are said to come true.

Thus, how the New Year will turn out is more a matter of eye-hand-mouth coordination skills than anything else. By contrast, making a list of resolutions for the New Year (a tradition rooted in Puritan beliefs, a quick internet search reveals) places the burden of the next twelve months' outcome smack on the person making the list, and his or her moral fortitude. Setting aside what the two traditions might indicate about Spanish versus U.S. culture, the point is that I was unfamiliar with the idea of New Year resolutions as a child and young adult (although I hear that the concept, just like the notion of Halloween and Black Friday, is catching up across the Atlantic). Indeed, I had never written down a list of New Year resolutions... but just now I did for the first time ever.

The reason for the change? A paper just published in *Psychological Science*, with the enticing title "Put Your Imperfections behind You: Temporal Landmarks Spur Goal Initiation When They Signal New

Beginnings." A team of scientists from Washington University in St. Louis and the University of Pennsylvania set out to explore, in a series of experiments, why certain dates are more likely to inspire people to pursue their goals (start a new diet, give up smoking, ramp up their exercise regime). The scientists also asked whether people's strengthened resolve at particular temporal landmarks might be linked to their distancing themselves, psychologically, from their past, imperfect personas.

The researchers reasoned that salient temporal landmarks may spur goal initiation because they signal new beginnings (i.e. an opportunity to clean the slate and start from scratch). Such transition points include those in social timetables (the start of holidays, the beginning of the New Year), as well as personal life events, recurring (a birthday, a wedding anniversary) and not (a first date, going away to college, moving to a new city). Previous research had already shown that temporal landmarks serve as dividers between people's past, present, and future selves, weakening the psychological connection between them.

[As an aside, I find the last point fascinating: most of us experience a sense of continuity between who we are now and who we used to be. Even if the actual connection between our past and present selves is tenuous, our autobiographical memories provide usually inescapable evidence that, however different we may feel from the way we were at the age of 4 or 14, we are the same people nevertheless. Even though personal continuity may be a necessary, adaptive illusion, it can nevertheless prevent us from effecting major changes in our behavior ("This is who I am, so there's nothing I can do to change"). Yet, if the construct of a continuous self does weaken at major temporal milestones, such dates may allow the possibility of new and improved selves to be born)].

The scientists further hypothesized that the more starkly the temporal milestone marked the start of a new period, the more psychological distance it should create between past and present selves. The disconnect between the current self and past imperfections could promote goal initiation in multiple ways: boosting perceived self-efficacy, lessening perceived self-tarnish from recent failures, and creating a clean slate–so that deviating from the goal (say, cheating on one's diet) may loom much more disastrous than if it is just one more in a long list of infractions.

Throughout the experimental series, the researchers found that temporal landmarks associated with new beginnings (i.e. both the start of a season and that of an academy period) were more appealing choices to jumpstart habit changes than ordinary dates. Consistent with these findings, Jewish participants also felt that the same date (October 5th) was more indicative of a new beginning when described as "the first day after Yom Kippur" than as "the 278th day of the year."

The scientists then recruited a sample of participants that planned to pursue a goal in the New Year. They asked half of the participants to write three to five reasons why the New Year felt meaningful to them, and the other half to write three to five reasons why this New Year felt ordinary to them. The people that wrote reasons why the New Year felt like a new beginning spent more time in goal-related activities, such as goal-tracking Web sites and written information on how people may increase their chances of achieving their goals.

Next, the team set out to exclude the alternate possibility that people simply start new activities (congruent or incongruent with achieving goals) at temporal milestones. Here, experimental participants were given a fictional scenario, in which a Chinese man named Chang turned 36 (which the researchers described as the beginning of a new zodiac cycle to only half of the participants). Chang's birthday coincided with a visit to the doctor, in which he learned that he was at high risk of lung cancer and should avoid smoking. Half the total number of participants were told that Chang had been wanting to quit smoking for several years but never succeeded. The other half read that Chang had been tempted to start smoking but had never done it. Participants who were familiar with the Chinese zodiac calendar thought that Chang would be more motivated to quit smoking than those who were unfamiliar.

In contrast, both the participants that were familiar and unfamiliar with the Chinese zodiac calendar thought it very unlikely that Chang would be motivated to start smoking when he had not done so in the past. These results indicated that major temporal milestones selectively spur the adoption of behaviors that are goal-congruent, rather than the adoption of *any* new behaviors.

Finally, the researchers asked if one reason that people's motivation to pursue goals increases at temporal landmarks can be that, at such points in time, they feel more psychologically separated from their past imperfect selves. To answer this question, they presented study participants with a fictional scenario in which half of the subjects had to imagine moving to a new city for the first time in nine years (new-beginning condition). The other half had to imagine moving cities for the ninth consecutive time in nine years (control condition). Then they had to rate, in various ways, the psychological distance that they felt between their present selves (after the move) and their imperfect past selves. Participants that had to imagine moving for the first time in nine years felt more disconnected from their imperfect past selves than participants who imagined moving every year for the past nine years. Participants in the new-beginning condition also said they would be more motivated to tackle personal goals than those in the control condition.

The combined results indicated that temporal landmarks that signal new beginnings cause people to engage in activities designed to facilitate goal initiation, and to predict higher motivation to pursue goals, both for themselves and for other people. This renewed impetus to tackle goals derives in part from the psychological disconnect between a person's current self and his/her past inferior self that occurs at major temporal landmarks.

In light of this research, I have been pondering my failure to maintain certain exercise habits during the past year. Can I use the 2016 temporal landmark to get myself to exercise three times a week? Yeah–that's it! I hereby choose to believe that the major culprit for my former noncompliance was my past inferior self. I am positive that that weak-willed malingerer is miles and miles apart from my much enhanced new 2016 personality upgrade. So, for the first time ever, I have written a long list of New Year resolutions. I have also orchestrated an extended discussion with my immediate family about why 2016 feels so much like a new start. You know, to lock in the change.

The views expressed are those of the author(s) and are not necessarily those of Scientific American.

About the Author

Susana Martinez-Conde is a professor of ophthalmology, neurology, and physiology and pharmacology at SUNY Downstate Health Sciences University in Brooklyn, N.Y. She is author of the Prisma Prize–winning Sleights of Mind, *along with Stephen Macknik and Sandra Blakeslee, and of* Champions of Illusion, *along with Stephen Macknik.*

How to Be an Optimal Human

By Scott Barry Kaufman

What does it take to be an optimal human being?

Throughout history there has been much speculation. For Aristotle, the highest human good was eudaimonia. For Carl Rogers, it was the "fully functioning person". For Abraham Maslow, it was "self-actualization". For Erik Erickson, it was wisdom and integrity. For Erich Fromm, it was about having a "being" orientation (in which you value personal growth and love) instead of a "doing" orientation (in which you value material possessions and status).

But are these theories right? Over the past 30 years or so, a number of contemporary psychologists have experimentally tested various aspects of these theories, and we are starting to get a clearer picture of those who seem to be well-integrated, thriving human beings.* Here I will offer some science-informed prescriptions, in the hopes that it helps you in your own journey toward greater health, growth, and happiness.

1. Strive to Balance Your Basic Needs

It turns out that Abraham Maslow was pretty spot on with his proposed list of basic needs (although he did miss a few). A large number of studies have confirmed that humans across cultures have a need for autonomy, competence, relatedness, security, and self-esteem.

Those with high autonomy feel as though they are authors of their own lives, and feel able to freely express their values and develop their identity, talents and interests. Those high in competence and self-esteem feel as though they are making good progress toward their goals, and are receiving positive regard from others. Those high in relatedness and security feel socially connected to others and feel as though they are part of a safe community.

The key prescription here is to strive to balance these basic needs. Without balance, it will be difficult to achieve optimal functioning. For instance, think of the workaholic who is high in autonomy, security, competence, and self-esteem, but has very little social connection with others. Despite high achievement, this person will most likely be prone to feelings of alienation, sadness, and loneliness. As Sheldon notes, "obtaining much need satisfaction may be a shorthand route to optimal human being."

2. Set and Make Efficient Progress Toward Self-Concordant Goals

On the path toward optimal functioning, you will want to set and pursue goals as effectively as possible. It's important that you feel as though your self is constantly in steady forward motion.

But here's the thing: this alone will not suffice. Mindlessly setting and efficiently achieving goals will not, by itself, make you happy, healthy, or fulfilled. It's important that the goals that you set have high "self-concordance." People with high self-concordant goals have identified goals that are consistent with their identity, basic needs, personality, and talents.

In one study, pursuing goals for self-concordant reasons (because one enjoys and fully identifies with the goals) predicted greater need satisfaction and well-being than pursuing goals for non-concordant reasons (because of environmental pressures and/or internal compulsions). Therefore, for optimal functioning, behavior must be both effective *and* consistent with inherent basic needs and growth tendencies.

You can imagine a situation in which a highly smart and capable person is forced to go into a field (e.g., medicine) by his parents, but he doesn't get a sense of autonomy because of the long work hours, and misses his friends. So this isn't the optimal condition for him in his life. Or consider the person who has the clear talent for something as a child (e.g., playing violin), but never really enjoys what she is doing and never really views it as part of her identity. This, too, will not lead to optimal health, growth, and happiness.

Which is why it's very important to...

3. Choose Your Goals and Social Roles Wisely

What kind of goals are more likely to lead to optimal functioning? The research suggests that Fromm was right. Setting *extrinsic* goals (such as money, beauty and status) tend to make you less happy, whereas attaining *intrinsic* goals (such as intimacy, community, and personal growth) tend to lead to enhanced well-being. It's also important to choose social roles that best fit your unique personality.

Often we have *multiple* goals, however. Which is why we should...

4. Strive Toward Personality Integration

Many of the great humanistic psychologists, such as Rogers and Maslow (but also William James and Carl Jung), frequently talked about the importance of achieving personality integration. The latest psychology of goals confirms these seminal thinkers were right.

In one study, Ken Sheldon and Tim Kasser measured personality integration by seeing how much people's goals were congruent with each other and with basic needs, and how much the goals were chosen freely and were expressive of intrinsic values such as as growth, intimacy, and community. They found that the extent to which people's goals were integrated, the more they felt as though their strivings originated from their own interests and choices, and the more they felt engaged in meaningful activities such as helping others or pondering the future. Integrated people also reported higher levels of self-esteem, openness to new experiences, vitality, satisfaction with life, self-actualization, positive moods, and fewer negative moods. Integrated people also felt more positive about their different life roles and felt all of these roles were in harmony with one another.

Clearly, having an integrated personality brings with it a whole nexus of positive, adaptive outcomes. However, sometimes you (or others) might keep getting in the way of adaptive integration. Which is why you often will want to...

5. Work Toward Modifying Problematic Aspects of Yourself or Your World

There's a lot of advice out there to just "be yourself," or be "true to yourself." But this advice is really quite misguided. Not all of our potentialities will help us make progress toward our self-concordant goals. Some aspects of our personality, like anxiety or disagreeableness, can downright get in the way of making progress toward becoming an optimal human. So the advice here is to not mindlessly accommodate your entire nature, but work on bringing out the character strengths and virtues that will best help you achieve your self-concordant goals. This may require learning self-regulation strategies and learning more about your character strengths.

To be clear: Even though your personality is influenced by your genes, this does *not* mean that personality change isn't possible. In this review, the researchers make a good case that substantial changes in personality and happiness are indeed possible through changes in activities and behaviors. Such changes that can cause substantial changes in personality and happiness include setting and pursuing self-concordant goals, adopting positive strategies for coping with stress, adopting positive mindsets and attitudes, and adopting behaviors specifically known to increase happiness.

Sometimes you don't just want to work on modifying your personality, however. Sometimes you also want to modify your *culture*. As Sheldon notes, "be prepared to go against the cultural grain when necessary." Sometimes being an iconoclast may be beneficial to optimal functioning. Some of the most important revolutionaries derived great meaning (but not necessarily happiness) by rebelling against the status quo of their culture.

Ultimately though, you need to own yourself and your decisions. Why is why it's important to...

6. Take Responsibility for Your Goals and Choices

A common theme of the great existential philosophers, such as Jean-Paul Sartre, is that we must take responsibility for our choices. Similarly, Sheldon argues that optimal humans take an "intentional attitude" toward life, by consciously aligning their sense of self with their life choices. Sheldon argues for the importance of taking ownership of your self-concordant goals, as only you can truly alter yourself and your life, and follow-through on your initiatives with good faith.

After making a decision about which goal you wish to adopt, embrace the goal with all of your being, and consciously align your identity with the goal (it's the difference between "I like writing science fiction" and "I *am* a science fiction writer").

However, this doesn't mean you must be rigid in maintaining your self-concordant goals at all costs. Sometimes we take ownership over goals that end up working against our ever evolving identity, personality, talents, and basic needs. Which leads us to #7...

7. Listen to Your 'Organismic Valuing Process' and Be Prepared to Change Your Goals If It Seems Necessary

Central to Carl Rogers' notion of the fully functioning person was getting in touch with your "organismic valuing process" (OVP). According to Rogers, the path toward becoming a fully functioning person requires developing increasing trust in your own ability to know what is important to you, and what is essential for you to live a more fulfilling life. Rogers believed that the OVP evolved to help us evaluate our experiences and actions and to determine whether they are leading us toward self-actualization. As Sheldon notes, all of us have experienced that "nagging sense that something isn't right". Optimal humans listen to that nagging.

Research suggests that Rogers was right. Sheldon and colleagues assessed changes in people's goals and values over time. They found that people tend to move toward intrinsic goals (e.g., emotional intimacy, personal growth, societal contribution) and/or away from extrinsic goals (e.g., material possessions, physical attractiveness, social popularity) over an extended period of time. They also found that decisions regarding extrinsic goals took longer, suggesting that the OVP causes people to pay particular attention when growth-relevant decisions have to be made. The researchers conclude: "People really do have some idea about what kind of goals are most likely to be beneficial for their subjective well-being, presumably because they possess an OVP."

Bottom line: trust yourself to abandon a goal if it is no longer appropriate for your growth. Constantly consult your OVP when making choices about which goals to adopt. You, and you alone, have the power to revise your goals as a result of new information. When the self-concordant goals you've adopted become inappropriate to your evolving self, personality, or basic needs, make a change.

It should be noted that Rogers believed that the OVP doesn't only motivate self-enhancement but can also motivate more prosocial motivations, given supportive conditions. In support of this idea, research has indeed found that a strong intrinsic goal pursuit is associated with prosocial behaviors such as helping others in our everyday lives.

Which leads us to the last suggestion for becoming an optimal human...

8. Transcend Your Self

In *Man's Search for Meaning*, Viktor Frankl notes that:

> *Being human always points, and is directed, to something or someone, other than oneself–be it a meaning to fulfill or another human being to encounter. The more one forgets himself–by*

giving himself to a cause to serve or another person to love–the more human he is and the more he actualizes himself. What is called self-actualization is not an attainable aim at all, for the simple reason that the more one would strive for it, the more he would miss it. In other words, self-actualization is possible only as a side-effect of self-transcendence.

Likewise, during the very end of his life, Maslow proposed a new need right above self-actualization: *self-transcendence*. He realized that many of his self-actualizers weren't self-transcenders, and even some of his self-transcenders weren't even self-actualizers. (Unfortunately, most introductory psychology textbooks don't mention Maslow's updated theory).

Sheldon suggests that becoming an optimal human can be facilitated by striving toward higher-level goals that allow you to serve something beyond yourself. In addition to personality integration, try integrating yourself into the larger social systems in which you are embedded. Don't just search for things that are useful to you, but be useful to others.

What Do You Get When These Are All Aligned?

This is by no means an exhaustive list of suggestions for how to be an optimal human being, but it's a good start. In sum:

1. Try to balance your basic needs for autonomy, competence, relatedness, security, and self-esteem.
2. Choose a goal that is in line with these needs, as well as your deepest self and talents, and that helps the larger community or world.
3. Learn self-regulatory strategies and cultivate your character strengths to make efficient progress toward your goals.
4. Constantly listen to your organismic valuing process, and modify your goals and personality as necessary.

Work toward all of this, and you will be well on your way to becoming the person you are capable of becoming.

** In his scholarly book* Optimal Human Being, *psychologist Ken Sheldon does a nice job summarizing and integrating a large number of these studies. Also, I recommend reading the writings of the following researchers, who have significantly advanced our knowledge of the optimal person: Charles Carver, Edward Deci, Edward Diener, Robert Biswas-Diener, Angela Duckworth, Robert Emmons, Adam Grant, Heidi Grant Halvorson, Todd Kashdan, Dacher Keltner, Art Markman, Richard Ryan, Carol Ryff, Michael Scheier, Martin Seligman, Ken Sheldon, and Heidi Wayment.*

*** To be clear, by "optimal," psychologists are not making a value judgment, or saying you should definitely live your life a certain way. It's up to you how you wish to live your life. Instead, what they are saying is that those who seem to have optimal health, growth, and happiness do tend to have certain characteristics, and therefore we have a lot we can learn from such individuals.*

The views expressed are those of the author(s) and are not necessarily those of Scientific American.

About the Author

Scott Barry Kaufman, Ph.D., is a humanistic psychologist exploring the depths of human potential. He has taught courses on intelligence, creativity, and well-being at Columbia University, NYU, the University of Pennsylvania, and elsewhere. He hosts The Psychology Podcast, *and is author and/or editor of nine books, including* Transcend: The New Science of Self-Actualization, Wired to Create: Unravelling the Mysteries of the Creative Mind *(with Carolyn Gregoire), and* Ungifted: Intelligence Redefined. *In 2015, he was named one of "50 Groundbreaking Scientists who are changing the way we see the world" by* Business Insider. *Find out more at http://ScottBarryKaufman.com. He wrote the extremely popular* Beautiful Minds *blog for* Scientific American *for close to a decade.*

Section 3: The Meeting of Procrastination and Motivation

Procrastinating Again? How to Kick the Habit

By Trisha Gura

Raymond, a high-powered attorney, habitually put off returning important business calls and penning legal briefs, behaviors that seriously threatened his career. Raymond (not his real name) sought help from clinical psychologist William Knaus, who practices in Longmeadow, Mass. As a first step, Knaus gave Raymond a two-page synopsis of procrastination and asked him to read it "and see if the description applied." Raymond agreed to do so on a flight to Europe. Instead he watched a movie. He next vowed to read it the first night at his hotel, but he fell asleep early. After that, each day brought something more compelling to do. In the end, Knaus calculated that the lawyer had spent 40 hours delaying a task that would have taken about two minutes to complete.

Almost everyone occasionally procrastinates, which University of Calgary economist Piers Steel defines as voluntarily delaying an intended course of action despite expecting to be worse off for the delay. But like Raymond, a worrisome 15 to 20 percent of adults, the "maana procrastinators," routinely put off activities that would be better accomplished ASAP. And according to a 2007 meta-analysis by Steel, procrastination plagues a whopping 80 to 95 percent of college students, whose packed academic schedules and frat-party-style distractions put them at particular risk.

Procrastination does not mean deliberately scheduling less critical tasks for later time slots. The term is more apt when a person fails to adhere to that logic and ends up putting off the tasks of *greater* importance or urgency. That is, if just thinking about tomorrow's job pricks the hair on the back of your neck or compels you to do something more trivial, you are probably procrastinating.

A penchant for postponement takes its toll. Procrastination carries a financial penalty, endangers health, harms relationships and ends careers. "Procrastination undermines well-being on a wide scale," notes psychologist Timothy A. Pychyl, director of the Procrastination Research Group at Carleton University in Ottawa. Nevertheless, recent work hints at potential upsides to this otherwise bad habit: perpetual foot-draggers seem to benefit emotionally from their trademark tactics, which support the human inclination to avoid the disagreeable.

Procrastination is learned, but certain hardwired personality traits increase the likelihood that a person will pick up the habit. "Procrastination is a dance between the brain and the situation," Pychyl says. That nature-and-nurture view is part of a new line of research into the process and prevention of procrastination. Understanding why people put off projects has led to strategies for helping all of us get and stay on task.

Built-in Bias

Procrastination is as old as humans are. For people living in agrarian societies, a late-planted crop could mean starvation. Thus, our ancestors, including Greek poet Hesiod in 800 b.c., equated procrastination with sin or sloth. The industrial revolution may have facilitated the practice of putting off important jobs. Technical advance brings some protection from the forces of storms and famine as well as an increase in leisure time, in consumer goods and in the number of possible *choices* of activities. Contemporary society offers a surfeit of distractions, including computer games, television and electronic messaging–not to mention cars and planes to take us to more stuff to see and do–all enticing us to move off task.

Succumbing to such enticements can be costly. Experts estimate that 40 percent of people have experienced a financial loss because of procrastination, in some cases severe. In 2002 Americans overpaid $473 million in taxes as a result of rushing and consequent errors. And Americans' dearth of retirement savings can be attributed, in part, to people putting off putting away cash.

Procrastination can also endanger health: after screening more than 19,800 people for high cholesterol, epidemiologist Cynthia Morris and her colleagues at the Oregon Health and Science University reported in 1990 that 35 percent of those who learned they had elevated cholesterol put off consulting a physician for at least five months. In 2006 psychologist Fuschia Sirois of the University of Windsor in Ontario reported in a study of 254 adults that procrastinators had higher stress levels and more acute health problems than did individuals who completed jobs in a timely manner. The procrastinators also received less frequent medical and dental checkups and had more household accidents, a result of putting off dull jobs such as changing smoke detector batteries.

Task aversiveness is one of the main external triggers for procrastination. Who puts off doing what she loves? According to Steel's meta-analysis, half of the college students surveyed cited the nature of the task itself as the reason they put it off. Undoubtedly, few leap at the chance to write a dissertation about nematode reproduction or clean out the garage. "Procrastination is about not having projects in your life that really reflect your goals," Pychyl says.

The amount of time before a project's due date also influences the tendency to procrastinate. In particular, people are more likely to dawdle when the deadline is far away. The reason for this lies in a phenomenon known as temporal delay, which means the closer a person gets to a reward (or a feeling of accomplishment), the more valuable the reward seems and hence the less likely he is to put off performing the work needed to earn it. In other words, immediate gratification is more motivating than are prizes or accolades to be accrued in the distant future.

Such a preference may have a strong evolutionary basis. The future, for those in the Stone Age, was unpredictable at best. "Thus, there was truth to the saying 'a bird in the hand is worth two in the bush,' " Pychyl says. "For survival, humans have brains with a procrastination bias built in."

In 2004 neuroscientist Barry Richmond and his colleagues at the National Institute of Mental Health reported finding a biological basis for this bias. Richmond's team first trained monkeys to release a lever whenever a spot on a computer screen turned from red to green. As the monkeys continued to correctly let go of the lever, a gray bar increased in brightness, letting the animals know they were getting closer to a reward, a juice treat. Like human procrastinators, the animals slacked off during early trials, making lots of errors. But when the juice reward came closer, the animals stayed on task and made fewer mistakes.

Richmond's team hypothesized that the neurotransmitter dopamine, which transmits feelings of reward, might underlie this behavior. Working with Richmond, molecular geneticist Edward Ginns used a molecular decoy called DNA antisense to partially shut down production of a receptor for dopamine in a region of the monkeys' brains called the rhinal cortex that associates visual cues with reward. The treatment diminished dopamine's effects to the point that the monkeys could no longer predict when any given trial would earn them a juice treat. Thus, they hedged their bets, working hard all the time as if "they are always one trial away from the penultimate," Richmond says.

But not all the monkeys with diminished dopamine responses behaved with the same intensity. Some remained mellow after the dopamine-depressing treatment, failing to put in much effort even as the time to reward narrowed. That observation speaks to individuality in procrastination: some of us are more prone to it than others.

Getting Personal

At the end of the 20th century, psychologists began studying the so-called big five personality traits that blend to describe any human being: conscientiousness, agreeableness, neuroticism, openness and extroversion. According to Steel, the extent to which a person displays each of these traits helps to determine that individual's proclivity to procrastinate.

The characteristic most strongly linked to procrastination is conscientiousness—or lack thereof. A highly conscientious person is dutiful, organized and industrious. Therefore, someone who is not conscientious has a high probability of procrastinating. A person who is impulsive also is a procrastinator at risk. "People who are impulsive can't shield one intention from another," Pychyl says. So they are easily diverted by temptations—say, the offer of a beer—that crop up in the middle of a project such as writing a term paper.

Procrastination can also stem from anxiety, an offshoot of neuroticism. Procrastinators postpone getting started because of a fear of failure (*I am so worried that I will bungle this assignment*), the fear of ultimately making a mistake (*I need to make sure the outcome will be perfect*), and the fear of success (*If I do well, people will expect more of me all the time. Therefore, I'll put the assignment off until the last minute, do it poorly, and people won't expect so much of me*).

These personality traits, as well as less influential ones, play out in particular situations in conjunction with the environment. Researchers are now trying to capture that nature-nurture interaction to unify existing procrastination theories and to predict who is likely to procrastinate under what circumstances. Steel has derived a mathematical formula that defines "utility," that is, how desirable a task is for an individual. To determine a task's utility and therefore how likely a person is to do it right away, Steel puts together four basic factors, expectancy (E), value (V), the delay until reward or punishment (D), and personal sensitivity to delay (P), in the following equation:

$$U = (E \times V) / (P \times D)$$

When a person expects to succeed at or values a particular task, she is more likely to do it. Hence, a higher number for expectancy or value will increase utility. On the other hand, if a reward or punishment lies far in the future or a person is particularly "sensitive," meaning distractible, impulsive or lacking in self-control, he is less likely to do the task, at least on time. Thus, sensitivity to delay and delay itself decrease the utility of a task and lead to procrastination.

Several scientists take issue with the idea that complex human behavior can be defined by a mathematical formula. "It leads you to believe that if I put numbers in there," Pychyl says, "I could tell you what you will be doing next Friday." Nevertheless, Steel's equation is an initial attempt to unify various motivational and psychological theories of procrastination and to provide a framework for future research.

The Psychology of Delay

Instead of measuring personality traits and solving formulas, some researchers prefer to tease out the psychology behind the behavior. Two key elements in the urge to let projects slide are an uneasy feeling about an activity and a desire to avoid that discomfort. "A procrastinator says, 'I feel lousy about a task,'" Pychyl explains, "and thus walks away to feel better." Psychologist Joseph Ferrari of DePaul University has coined "avoidance procrastinator" to describe a person for whom avoidance is the prime motivator.

Another psychological driver is indecision. An "indecisive procrastinator" cannot make up her mind about executing a task. Say a woman intends to visit her mother in the hospital. Rather than simply grabbing the keys and heading out, the indecisive procrastinator starts debating whether to drive or to take the train. *The train is a hassle, but parking is expensive and I'll have to drive back at rush hour. But then again, the train will be packed, too.* The internal debate continues until enough time passes that visiting hours are over.

A third oft-cited explanation for unreasonable delay is arousal. The "arousal procrastinator" swears that he works best under pressure, loving–perhaps needing–the rush of a last-minute deadline to get started. Such a person believes procrastinating affords a "peak" or "flow" experience, defined by psychologist Mihly Cskszentmihlyi of the Drucker School of Management at Claremont Graduate

University as being completely involved in an activity for its own sake. Time disappears. The ego dissolves.

But procrastination does not facilitate flow, according to social scientist Eunju Lee of Halla University in South Korea. In 2005 Lee reported surveying 262 students and finding that procrastinators tended to have *fewer*, not more, flow experiences. After all, a person must be able to let go of herself to "get lost" in an experience, and procrastinators are generally self-conscious individuals who have trouble doing that.

Nor is the thrill of a looming deadline an actual reason people put off uninviting jobs. Pychyl and his graduate student Kyle Simpson measured traits associated with arousal, including thrill seeking and extraversion, in students who often procrastinated. In Simpson's unpublished doctoral thesis, Pychyl and Simpson show that neither of these qualities accounted for the dawdling the students reported. Thus, procrastinators are probably not really in need of arousal, Pychyl says, but use the belief *I need the pressure of a last-minute deadline* to justify dragging their feet, which they do for other reasons, such as circumventing unpleasantness.

Other procrastinators strategically delay projects to excuse poor performance, should it occur. They tell themselves or others, "I could have done better if I had started earlier." Such a strategy might, in some cases, serve as a shield for a fragile ego.

Tricks of the Trade

Procrastination is not always so maladaptive. In a 2007 survey of 67 self-described procrastinators among college students, psychologist Gregory Schraw of the University of Nevada, Las Vegas, and his colleagues learned that these students found creative ways of making their bad habit work for them. For example, many students only took classes in which the professor offered a detailed syllabus rather than just a rough sketch of the assignments. Such specificity allowed for "planned" procrastination: the students could schedule how to delay their course work and thereby afford maximum time for more enticing activities.

To cope with the guilt and anxiety brought on by waiting until the last minute, some students acquired all the books for an assignment as soon as it was given and placed them on a shelf. The students said that by shelving the books they "shelved" their discomforting thoughts about the task. They also fended off guilt by telling themselves, "Hey, at least I got the books." Then, 48 hours before the project was due, the procrastinator dusted off the books and bad feelings and worked in a frenzy to get the assignment done. As a result, the students did the maximum amount of work in a minimum amount of time–with a minimal amount of pain.

So although these students were still putting off the work longer than they should, they were nonetheless managing to finish their assignment while maintaining their sanity. Schraw emphasizes that his work is not meant to advocate procrastination but to point out that the practice can engender some useful survival skills such as tactical planning to complete a task in limited time and with a minimum amount of stress. "The moral of the story is that people procrastinate so they can lead a better mental life," Schraw says.

Preventing Procrastination

Not all experts agree with Schraw. Indeed, Steel's meta-analysis suggests that 95 percent of procrastinators would like to break the habit but cannot, because it has become automatic and ingrained. "Habits become nonconscious brain processes," Pychyl says. "When procrastination becomes chronic, a person is, essentially, running on autopilot."

Some experts suggest replacing the reflex to postpone with time-stamped prescriptions for action. Psychologist Peter Gollwitzer of New York University and the University of Konstanz in Germany advises creating "implementation intentions," which specify where and when you will perform a specific behavior. So rather than setting a vague goal such as "I will get healthy," set one with its implementation, including timing, built in–say, "I will go to the health club at 7:30 a.m. tomorrow."

Setting such specific prescriptions does appear to inhibit the tendency to procrastinate. In 2008 psychologist Shane Owens and his colleagues at Hofstra University demonstrated that procrastinators who formed implementation intentions were nearly eight times as likely to follow through on a commitment than were those who did not create them. "You have to make a specific commitment to a time and place at which to act beforehand," Owens says. "That will make you more likely to follow through."

Smart scheduling can also thwart procrastination. In an experiment published in 2002 Duke University behavioral economist Dan Ariely, then at the Massachusetts Institute of Technology, and marketing professor Klaus Wertenbroch of INSEAD, a business school with campuses in France and Singapore, asked students in an executive-education class to set their own deadlines for the three papers due that semester. Ariely and Wertenbroch set penalties for papers turned in after the self-imposed deadlines. Despite the penalties, 70 percent of the students chose deadlines spaced out over the semester, rather than clustering them all at the end. What is more, those who set the early deadlines scored better, on average, than did students in a comparable class in which Ariely set one due date for all three papers at the end of the semester. Such planning can buck any inclination to put off the work. "The deadlines made them better performers," Ariely says.

More simply, Pychyl advises procrastinators to "just get started." The anticipation of the task often is far worse than the task turns out to be. To demonstrate this fact, his group, in work that appeared in 2000, gave 45 students pagers and checked in with the volunteers 40 times over five days to query them about their moods and how often they were putting off a task that had a deadline. "We found that when students actually do the task they are avoiding, their perceptions of the task change significantly. Many times, they actually enjoyed it."

In Raymond's case, getting to the task was, indeed, the hard part. Knaus helped him to do that by first determining the reason for his instinct to delay: Raymond feared being tested on the synopsis and looking foolish. So Knaus asked him to pick the lesser of two evils, doing his work—and risking imperfection—or avoiding difficult tasks and losing his job. When Knaus put it that way, the lawyer was able to "just grind it out." Instead of being fired, Raymond became a "superstar" at his firm.

Referenced

The Procrastination Workbook. William Knaus. New Harbinger Publications, 2002.

The Nature of Procrastination: A Meta-Analytic and Theoretical Review of Quintessential Self-Regulatory Failure. Piers Steel in *Psychological Bulletin*, Vol. 133, No. 1, pages 65–94; 2007.

Predictably Irrational. Dan Ariely. HarperCollins, 2008.

Don't Delay. Timothy A. Pychyl's blog in *Psychology Today* online: http://blogs.psychologytoday.com/blog/dont-delay

About the Author

Trisha Gura, based in Boston, is author of Lying in Weight: The Hidden Epidemic of Eating Disorders in Adult Women *(HarperCollins, 2007).*

Pre-Crastination: The Opposite of Procrastination

By David A. Rosenbaum and Edward A. Wasserman

Procrastination is a well-known and serious behavioral problem involving both practical and psychological implications. Taxpayers commonly put off submitting their annual returns until the last minute, risking mathematical errors in their frenzy to file. Lawmakers notoriously dawdle and filibuster before enacting sometimes rash and ill-advised legislation at the eleventh hour. And, students burn the midnight oil to get their term papers submitted before the impending deadline, precluding proper polishing and proofreading. For these reasons, we are cautioned not to procrastinate: *Don't put off until tomorrow what you can do today. He who hesitates is lost. Procrastination is the thief of time.*

However, the opposite of procrastination can also be a serious problem – a tendency we call "pre-crastination." Pre-crastination is the inclination to complete tasks quickly just for the sake of getting things done sooner rather than later. People answer emails immediately rather than carefully contemplating their replies. People pay bills as soon as they arrive, thus failing to collect interest income. And, people grab items when they first enter the grocery store, carry them to the back of the store, pick up more groceries at the back, and then return to the front of the store to pay and exit, thus toting the items farther than necessary. Familiar adages also warn of the hazards of pre-crastinating: *Measure twice, cut once. Marry in haste, repent at leisure. Look before you leap.*

We first found striking evidence of pre-crastination in a laboratory study exploring the economics of effort. College students were asked to carry one of a pair of buckets: one on the left side of a walkway and one on the right side of the same walkway. The students were instructed to carry whichever bucket seemed easier to take to the end of the walkway. We expected students to choose the bucket closer to the end because it would have to be carried a shorter distance. Surprisingly, they preferred the bucket closer to the starting point, actually carrying it farther. When asked why they did so, most students said something like, "I wanted to get the task done as soon as possible," even though this choice did not in fact complete the task sooner.

Nine experiments involving more than 250 students failed to reveal what might have been so compelling about picking up the nearer bucket. Although some hidden benefit may await discovery, a simple hypothesis is that getting something done, or coming closer to getting it done, is inherently rewarding. No matter how trivial the achievement, even something as inconsequential as picking up a bucket may serve as its own reward.

Is pre-crastination–exhibited by college students, bill payers, e-mailers, and shoppers–a symptom of our harried lives? The other study from our laboratories suggests it is not: that experiment was done with pigeons. The birds could earn food by pecking a touchscreen three times: first, into a square in the center of the screen; second, into the same square or into a square that randomly appeared to the left or right of it; and third, into a side square after a star appeared within it. Critically, food was given after the final peck regardless of whether the second peck struck the center square or the side square where the star would be presented. The pigeons directed their second peck to the side square, hence moving to the goal position as soon as they could even though there was no obvious or extra reward for doing so. Thus, the pigeons pre-crastinated.

Finding pre-crastination in the pigeon is particularly important because the evolutionary ancestors of pigeons and people went their separate ways 300 million years ago. Following a popular line of thinking in comparative psychology, the fact that both pigeons and people pre-crastinate suggests that this behavioral tendency may have emerged even earlier in phylogeny.

Why would our evolutionary kin have pre-crastinated, and why do we humans and our pigeon contemporaries do so now?

It is possible, as suggested above, that pre-crastination amounts to grabbing low-hanging fruit. If grain is nearby or if a bucket is close at hand, then it may be best to get it while it's available. Another explanation is that completing tasks immediately may relieve working memory. By doing a task right away, you don't have to remember to do it later; it can be taxing to keep future tasks in mind. Requiring people to delay performance of a task often worsens their performance of it. Yet, we doubt this is the whole story. Lifting a bucket doesn't tax working memory very much, and it's not obvious why directing the second peck to the future goal location would reduce the load on the pigeons' working memory. A simpler account is that task completion is rewarding in and of itself. Tasks that can be completed quickly woo us more than tasks that must delayed. All potential tasks, or their underlying neural circuits, compete for completion. Neural circuits for tasks that get completed may endure longer than neural circuits for tasks that don't.

Another benefit of completing tasks as soon as possible is to provide us with as much information as possible about the costs and benefits of task-related behaviors. Trial-and-error learning is the most reliable way we discover what does and doesn't succeed in everyday life. Such learning can even prompt practical behavioral innovations. Given these benefits, it may be better to gain experience from several trials than only a few.

Pre-crastination clearly adds to the challenge of coping with procrastination. Not only must procrastinators start sooner to begin tasks they'd rather defer, but they must also inhibit the urge to complete small, trivial tasks that bring immediate rewards just for being completed. The discovery of pre-crastination may suggest a way to counter the ills of procrastination. Break larger tasks into smaller ones. Such smaller tasks, when completed, will promote a sense of accomplishment, will bring one closer to the final goal, and, via trial-and-error learning, may support the discovery of even more adaptive or innovative ways of behaving.

About the Author

David A. Rosenbaum, a professor of psychology at Pennsylvania State University, is the author of It's a Jungle in There: How Competition and Cooperation in the Brain Shape the Mind *(Oxford University Press, 2014) and co-author of* MATLAB For Behavioral Scientists *(Routledge, 2015).*

Edward A. Wasserman, a professor of psychology at the University of Iowa, is the co-author of How Animals See the World *and* Oxford Handbook of Comparative Cognition *(both published by Oxford University Press, 2012).*

Sloth: To Stop Procrastinating, Focus on Emotions

By Sandra Upson

Timothy Pychyl, a psychologist at Carleton University, dotes on his eight huskies. On winter weekends he takes them dogsledding on the snow-covered trails near his house in Ottawa.

As the number of dogs has grown, though, so have the chores. Pychyl dreads one duty above all others: clipping their claws, all 150 (or so) of them.

"One of my dogs takes two or three people to pin him down, that's how much he doesn't like it," Pychyl recounts. Although he wants the dogs to be happy and healthy, when faced with spending a strenuous evening wrangling husky paws, he finds himself severely tempted to sink into the couch with a beer.

This trade-off is the essence of procrastination. We know what we want to do, yet we bellyache, sabotage ourselves and settle for second-rate mental diversions. Why?

The easy answer is that we prefer to seek fun things now rather than waiting for a distant payoff, even when that long-term reward is significantly greater. Yet that tendency fails to explain why we sometimes twiddle our thumbs but other times get down to business. "The 'why' is emotional processes," says psychologist Fuschia Sirois of Bishop's University in Quebec. "We face emotional conflict and tension, and one way to resolve that is to procrastinate."

Recent research suggests that feeling insecure or gloomy can make us more likely to procrastinate because yielding to our impulses offers an emotional boost. To morph from couch potato to action hero, we must learn to harness the subtle lifts and dips in our emotions. Transforming an initial aversion into a source of motivation can help us dodge temptations and chase bigger, bolder dreams.

Deconstructing Delay

Procrastination is an engine of regret, one that has steamrolled human accomplishment since the dawn of civilization. As early as 800 B.C., Greek poet Hesiod offered a now familiar piece of advice: "Do not put off your work until tomorrow and the day after." We can procrastinate about anything: work, exercise, starting a diet or sending a birthday card. More formally, it has been defined as the voluntary delay of any action that we realize we ought to pursue now.

Perhaps because of its universality, the phenomenon is also the frequent butt of jokes–the procrastinators club that never met, the book on procrastination that was never written. One writer even cited fake procrastination research in a journal article: two fictional scientists named Stilton and Edam used cheese to observe procrastination in mice. And Saint Augustine, during his hedonistic youth in the fourth century, famously prayed, "Grant me chastity and continence–but not yet."

For habitual practitioners, though, the reality is anything but humorous. Frequent dawdlers tend to harbor self-critical thoughts and wrestle with depression and anxiety. They are consistently found to yield to impulses more often than other people. Now researchers are discovering a causal link among procrastination, impulsivity and mood. "A lot of the literature says that [such people] have higher levels of depression, anxiety, etcetera," Sirois observes. "It's not just about being driven purely by pleasure seeking but about avoiding negative emotions."

When chronic procrastinators are queried about their thoughts, they tend to share snippets of a dark, gloom-ridden internal dialogue. "I'm too stupid for this," they say, or "If I can't complete this paper, everything else I've done is meaningless." In one case study, an accountant named Tom procrastinated so much that he failed to file his own taxes. We may chuckle at the irony, but when asked how he felt about the situation, Tom said he felt defective, incompetent and pathetic.

Numerous studies by psychologist Roy F. Baumeister of Florida State University and his collaborators have demonstrated that negative emotions diminish self-control. Anxiety undermines diets as well as smokers' efforts to quit. When people feel upset, they are more likely to act aggressively, spend too much money or play games when they know they should be studying. Feeling down is also a strong predictor of relapse in a number of addictive behaviors, such as alcoholism and gambling.

A fundamental function of the brain is to regulate emotion, including dispelling negative feelings when they do not signal a threat to survival. At the sight of a disturbing image, for instance, we deflect our gaze. When preparing to give a talk, we try to look cool and collected as a way to quiet the turmoil inside. And it is no accident that after a breakup, some of us reach for a tub of ice cream. All three strategies serve to patch up psychological injury, just as we might bandage a cut.

Distraction, it turns out, is a fabulous way to cast off unwanted feelings. Students doodling in the margins of their notebooks might have discovered on their own what psychologists only recently have shown in the laboratory: that drawing can quell negative emotions not through its expressive power but by distracting us from our feelings. Not all diversions need be so active: another effective way of restoring self-control and a chipper mood is simply to take a nap—a tried-and-true tactic of procrastinating college students.

Turning the mind away from a dull or disturbing thought is one reason we dillydally, but other emotional processes may also be at work. Psychologists Jeffrey A. Hancock and Catalina L. Toma of the University of Wisconsin–Madison speculated that a bruised ego might compel someone to procrastinate as a way to repair his sense of self. After a setback at a meeting, a person who is feeling defeated might return to his desk, check the scores from last night's game and browse Facebook as a way to affirm, unconsciously, his feelings of social connectedness.

To test this idea, Hancock and Toma asked 86 study participants to prepare and deliver a short speech. Half the subjects then received criticism, whereas the rest heard neutral comments. The participants had the opportunity to either browse their own Facebook profile or engage in one of four other online diversions: watching YouTube videos, reading news, listening to music or playing video games. The results, published this year, showed that the people who weathered criticism were twice as likely to choose Facebook over the other online diversions as those receiving neutral feedback; the time spent on the social network seems to indeed repair mood. In a related experiment, in which ego-bruised participants viewed either their own Facebook profile or that of a stranger, Hancock and Toma found that people who checked out their own page dealt with the criticism better than those who visited the stranger's page. (They were more likely to assume responsibility and less inclined to blame others for the negative feedback.) Although you may think you procrastinate for no reason, the dawdling may be a subconscious move to self-affirm: to check in with the values and passions that shape your identity.

Other subtle emotion-regulation strategies also differentiate the doers from the dawdlers. Sirois investigated how procrastinators use a set of thoughts known as counterfactuals. These statements often begin with phrases such as "at least" or "if only"—for example, "at least I didn't crash the car!" or "if only I'd gotten a good night's sleep." Downward counterfactuals, which illustrate how things could have been worse, serve to elevate mood. Upward counterfactuals, which capture how we might have avoided a mistake, do the opposite.

In a study published in 2004 Sirois measured 80 students' tendency to procrastinate and then asked them to read a story that described what it might be like to watch one's house burn down. Afterward the participants wrote as many counterfactuals related to the tale as they could think of. As she discovered, the students who procrastinated more egregiously dreamed up more downward counterfactuals than those less prone to postponement. Sirois reasons that chronic idlers might be less resilient when beset by negative feelings, so their defense mechanisms kick in sooner. "There is a discomfort that comes when you approach a task that brings up insecurities, and for some people that is just not a place they like to be," Sirois reflects.

Getting to Work

One obstacle for any procrastination-beating technique is that managing our internal state–herding our thoughts and feelings so they align with our highest goals–often demands self-control, and this effort can leave us with less cognitive firepower for the tasks at hand. Resolving to not check e-mail for an hour, for example, can make you more likely to sneak into the kitchen for a bag of chips.

The idea that negative emotions drive procrastination has opened up new approaches for bolstering resilience. Several strategies that leave self-control intact are now emerging from the labs. They can help us tackle household chores, finish projects at work or finally make a date with the dentist. And, as I learned recently, they apply to the tardy disposal of a Christmas tree.

In April I found myself in the ridiculous position of having a tree, ornaments and all, firmly ensconced in my living room. That winter I had postponed tossing it out of a sense of sadness at condemning a perfectly good tree to the city dump. Plus it served nicely as a hat stand–not to mention ongoing storage for all those ornaments.

Suddenly it was March. In a blink another month passed, and my feelings started to shift. I dreaded lugging it out to the street for garbage collection. What would the neighbors think? I avoided entertaining visitors so that they could not mock my brittle Douglas fir. I was now hostage to the tree.

A shift in motivation eventually saved the day. Instead of dwelling on the potential for embarrassment, I focused on a dinner party I had agreed to host. I needed to get this tree out of my house to make room for friends, and tossing the fir became virtuous, not vexing. Without realizing it, I had tapped into one key strategy for overcoming procrastination: cognitive reappraisal.

Cognitive reappraisal is a deliberate move to change the meaning of a situation by altering our emotional response to it. In research published in 2012 psychologist James Gross of Stanford University and his colleagues set out to assess whether reappraisal could help us diffuse the allure of temptations without depleting self-control. In one of Gross's studies, 51 students were asked to memorize details about several wines while sitting in a room with distracting pictures, such as the posters and photographs that decorate dorm rooms. Half the students were prompted to view the activity as an opportunity to strengthen their memory, which could help them in college. The remaining participants, the control group, were simply instructed to do their best.

The researchers found that thinking of the task as self-improvement decreased the students' susceptibility to temptation and helped them remember more information about the wines. Several variations on this experiment similarly showed that reappraisal increases people's focus, enthusiasm and performance–three things most rueful procrastinators surely covet.

The finding is in line with prior work by two of Gross's co-authors on this study, Véronique Leroy and Jacques Grégoire of the Catholic University of Louvain in Belgium. They have shown that university students who routinely reappraise their emotional reactions tend to do better in school. As Gross explains, cognitive reappraisal "is a little like learning to surf. If you can harness the incredibly powerful force of your emotions, you'll have a lot more fun than if you're constantly turned around and around by them."

Pychyl overcame his aversion to trimming his huskies' claws by focusing on love and care. "There are other places in my inner landscape from which I can work," he muses. "My first emotions for a task are not the only emotions in me." He also breaks the chore down into smaller parts. He tells himself to take care of one animal and then permits himself to call it quits. Inevitably the job is not as bad as he imagines, and all 150 claws get clipped.

Another way to view an event more positively is to give yourself a break. Because procrastination seems to trigger harsh self-criticism, it may be self-reinforcing, sending us spiraling further downward. For this reason, Pychyl has highlighted the importance of self-forgiveness: a three-step process to reduce the emotional distress that procrastination stirs up. It entails acknowledging having made a mistake, weathering feelings of guilt and then experiencing a shift in motivation as self-punishment gives way to the positive feeling of self-acceptance.

To test the value of forgiveness, Pychyl and his colleagues gave 119 students in a class questionnaires measuring their tendency to procrastinate and either forgive or berate themselves for it. The students reported on their procrastination twice, both times before a midterm. Between the exams, they indicated how they felt about their performance.

The researchers discovered that the students who were kindest to themselves after procrastinating for the first midterm experienced fewer negative emotions and improved their study habits for the subsequent test. Conversely, students who continued beating themselves up for procrastinating not only felt worse but also perpetuated their mistakes for the second exam. Thus, the next time you miss a deadline because you stayed up late watching cat videos on YouTube, don't dwell on the mistake. Acknowledge your error and feelings of guilt, then move on.

A partial explanation for why criticism fuels procrastination may come from self-affirmation–the same strategy that sent people in Hancock and Toma's study scurrying to Facebook for a fix of pleasant feelings. That self-affirmation was unconscious, but it can also be deliberate.

This idea is based on the theory that humans are powerfully motivated to pursue self-worth. A suite of studies has made it clear that consulting our deepest values can free a person from defensive responses. Starting with work published in 2009, psychologist Kathleen D. Vohs of the University of Minnesota and her colleagues have consistently found that self-affirmation can restore self-control.

For example, one experiment looked at how well people stayed on task when they either did or did not self-affirm. The participants in this study first wore out their self-control with a cognitively draining task–watching a video and keeping their attention trained on a woman's face on the screen while ignoring words that popped up periodically. They then wrote about either a personal value of great importance to them or about Bill Gates. Those who wrote about their own values persisted almost twice as long at a subsequent boring activity than did the ones who pondered the billionaire. Vohs and her colleagues theorize that reflecting on our core convictions helps us see the bigger picture. "My own pet theory is that it stops people from evaluating themselves for a moment and gets them to focus descriptively on what matters in life," Vohs says. A simple strategy such as having photos of family on your desk can serve as a reminder of what counts most.

With self-control all stocked up, we can shift away from our inner environments and begin tailoring external circumstances instead. Ultimately, it seems, the key is not to constantly fight temptations but to learn to avoid as many of them as possible. In a 2012 study Baumeister, Vohs and their collaborators asked 205 people from the city of Würzburg in Germany to wear smartphones for a week. Periodic signals to the phones cued them to record any desires they were feeling at that moment. The psychologists found that people reported some kind of desire in response to a whopping half of the cues. About half of those desires conflicted with a goal or value.

Looking more closely at the data, the researchers observed a funny thing: participants who scored high in self-control reported far fewer conflicting temptations than people on the low end. Thus, self-control may not be the capacity for titanic acts of willpower but instead an ability to shape one's environment proactively through effective habits and routines.

So if you plan to exercise in the morning, tuck your keys into your shorts and lay out your shoes the night before. Stash the alarm clock across the room. The fewer obstacles, the fewer opportunities for negative emotions to arise. And when you encounter an urge to avoid doing what matters most, check in with your feelings first. They may govern the moment, but you can still rule the day.

Referenced

The Nature of Procrastination: A Meta-Analytic and Theoretical Review of Quintessential Self-Regulatory Failure. Piers Steel in *Psychological Bulletin*, Vol. 133, No. 1, pages 65–94; January 2007.

I'll Do It Tomorrow. Trisha Gura in *Scientific American Mind*, Vol. 19, No. 6, pages 26–33; December 2008/January 2009.

Everyday Temptations: An Experience Sampling Study of Desire, Conflict, and Self-Control. Wilhelm Hoffmann, Roy F. Baumeister, Georg Förster and Kathleen D. Vohs in *Journal of Personality and Social Psychology*, Vol. 102, No. 6, pages 1318–1335; June 2012.

Procrastination and the Priority of Short-Term Mood Regulation: Consequences for Future Self. Fuschia Sirois and Timothy Pychyl in *Social and Personality Psychology Compass*, Vol. 7, No. 2, pages 115–127; February 2013.

About the Author

Sandra Upson is managing editor of Scientific American Mind.

"Cognitive Prosthesis" Enhances Productivity

By Diana Kwon

Choosing between instant gratification and future benefit can easily lead to shortsighted decisions: streaming TV instead of going to the gym, for example, or scrolling through social media rather than working on a challenging project. "Because of this misalignment between immediate reward and long-term value, people often struggle to do what's best for them in the long run," says Falk Lieder, a cognitive scientist at the Max Planck Institute for Intelligent Systems in Tübingen, Germany.

To guide individuals toward optimal choices, Lieder and his colleagues designed a digital tool they call a "cognitive prosthesis." It helps to match a decision's immediate reward with its long-term worth–using artificial intelligence to augment human decision-making through a to-do list. The researchers developed a set of models and algorithms that consider various elements such as a list of tasks, an individual's subjective aversion to each and the amount of time available. The system then assigns reward points to each task in a way that is customized to encourage that person to complete them all.

"The idea was to turn the challenging projects that people pursue in the real world into a gamelike environment," Lieder says. "The point system [gives] people proximal, attainable goals that signal that they're making progress."

The team tested the setup in a series of experiments with human subjects. The results, published online in August in *Nature Human Behaviour,* revealed that the AI support system helped people make better, faster decisions and procrastinate less–and it made them more likely to complete all the assigned tasks. In one experiment, in which the researchers presented 120 participants with a list of several writing assignments, they found that 85 percent of individuals who used the tool completed all their tasks; the rate was only 56 percent for those not using it.

The difference in completion rates was "quite impressive," says Mike Oaksford, a psychologist at Birkbeck, University of London, who was not involved in the study. "That seems to me to be a convincing demonstration that procrastination is something that this strategy [can] help with quite a lot."

Lieder says one of the current tool's limitations is that it can handle only short to-do lists, so he and his team are trying to scale it up for a larger number of tasks. At the same time, they are working with a company called Complice to integrate the tool into an existing to-do list app. The researchers also plan to run field experiments to see how well their cognitive prosthesis fares in the real world.

About the Author

Diana Kwon is a freelance journalist who covers health and the life sciences. She is based in Berlin.

Why Do Today What You Can Put Off Until Tomorrow

By David Biello

I am a moderate procrastinator. Even when I believe that I would be best served by finishing a task (say, filing this story), I will occasionally put it off in favor of some short-term reward (like a much needed caffeine fix). This tendency on my part to delay what is in my long-term interest can now be explained by a simple mathematical equation, according to industrial psychologist Piers Steel of the University of Calgary.

Steel developed the equation U = E x V / I x D, where U is the desire to complete the task; E, the expectation of success; V, the value of completion; I, the immediacy of task; and D, the personal sensitivity to delay, as a way of mathematically mapping a given individual's procrastination response. So, for example, my desire to finish this article is influenced by my relative confidence in writing it well and the prospect of a paycheck as well as a looming deadline and my inherent desire to go home at the end of the day. "You're more likely to put something off if you're a very impulsive individual," Steel says. But, "if you only work at the last minute, time on task tells."

Of course, this does not explain why humans would procrastinate in the first place, but it is certainly not a new problem. The Greek poet Hesiod, writing in 800 BC, averred "a man who puts off work is always at handgrips with ruin" and the divine incarnation Krishna singled out procrastinators for special scorn in the *Bhagavad Gita.* Nor does it explain why procrastination seems to be on the rise–afflicting as many as 95 percent of students and at least 15 percent of adults, according to two recent surveys. Perhaps the answer lies in the cornucopia of distractions that surround us, ranging from YouTube on our computers to finally getting around to uncluttering our desks just when we should be writing that article. "We have a workplace that is motivationally toxic," Steel says. "Convenient access to inferior choices is decidedly inconvenient."

But the problem of procrastination, which Steel came to by suffering from a particularly acute case of it in his own schooling, may have broader applications. The equation to describe it, dubbed temporal motivational theory, may be applicable to the entire field of human motivation. "You can use it to predict stock prices and other theories of motivation, such as goalsetting, [which] can be derived from it," Steel notes. "Even the behavior of nations and groups can be better described by using this theory."

Insights into our procrastinating ways may help explain why humans struggle with long-term problems that require immediate solutions such as climate change and mounting public debt. And by reducing human motivation to a formula, powerful computer models can be put to work to predict our choices (and perhaps create avatars that will successfully mimic us in online worlds). "Modeling complex systems is something that we've done. We do it with the weather," Steel says. "This gives us the initial foundation to do it with people's personalities."

For my part, I hope that game designers and other modelers procrastinate on taking up this challenge, perhaps distracted by things like this news item or by the motivational tests Steel has devised. Already, one of his tests labeled me as a moderate procrastinator and delayed this story by a good 15 minutes. "Millions of people-hours are spent making [distractions] as succulent as possible," he adds. "There are so many ways we could do something else."

About the Author

David Biello is a contributing editor at Scientific American.

Training the Brain's Motivation Center

By Matthew A. Scult

My heart pounds as I sprint to the finish line. Thousands of spectators cheer as a sense of elation washes over me. I savor the feeling. But then, the image slowly fades away and my true surroundings come into focus. I am lying in a dark room with my head held firmly in place, inside an MRI scanner. While this might typically be unpleasant, I am a willing research study participant and am eagerly anticipating what comes next. I hold my breath as I stare at the bar on the computer screen representing my brain activity. Then the bar jumps. My fantasy of winning a race had caused the "motivation center" of my brain to surge with activity.

I am participating in a study about neurofeedback, a diverse and fascinating area of research that combines neuroscience and technology to monitor and modulate brain activity in real time. My colleagues, Katie Dickerson and Jeff MacInnes, in the Adcock Lab at Duke University, are studying whether people can train themselves to increase brain activity in a tiny region of the brain called the VTA. Notably, the VTA is thought to be involved in motivation–the desire to get something that you want. For example, if I told you that by buying a lottery ticket you would be guaranteed to win $1,000,000, you would probably be very motivated to buy the ticket and would have a spike in brain activity in this region of your brain. But while studies have shown that motivation for external rewards (like money) activate the VTA, until now, we didn't know whether people could internally generate a motivational state that would activate this brain region.

To see if people can self-activate the VTA, my colleagues are using neurofeedback, which falls under the broader umbrella of biofeedback. Biofeedback uses technology to give people information about the functioning of their bodies so that they can try to change their physiology. Studies on using the technique to control heart rate, breathing rate, muscle tension, and skin temperature have been around since the 1960s, and these types of biofeedback are often used to help people reduce anxiety, chronic pain, or psychological disorders, with varying degrees of efficacy.

The latest iteration of biofeedback is neurofeedback, which provides a person with information on their brain activity milliseconds to seconds after it happens. Neurofeedback can use either an EEG machine, which records the electrical activity of the brain and is very fast, but not very specific, or it can use functional magnetic resonance imaging (fMRI), which records changes in blood flow in the brain and can better target specific brain regions, but is slower. The fMRI version of the technology has been around since as early as 1995 and its potential is slowly being realized. Studies on rtfMRI (the rt stands for "real-time") have found that giving people feedback on their brain activity might be able to help them to control that activity. These studies both help us to better understand the functioning of the brain and can be used for clinical purposes. Perhaps the most common use to date has been for chronic pain, where people learn to decrease activation in regions of the brain that process pain perception.

The study I'm participating in is about using the technology to better understand the functioning of the VTA and its relationship with internally generated motivation, with potential for clinical applications down the road. In animal models, artificially affecting functioning of the VTA can affect how much an animal eats or drinks, and can even affect its emotional responses. If people could learn to activate their VTAs deliberately, it could have important applications to anything from helping someone stick to a diet to helping with psychological disorders.

Back in the fMRI, I lie on the uncomfortable scanner bed, looking up at the giant machine that reminds me of something I might encounter on a spaceship. Katie Dickerson's voice comes over the intercom and gives me suggestions of ways to try and activate my VTA. She says I could try to think of phrases, like "you can do it!" or "increase that signal!" and says that it might help to think of the task as a fun game. So I think "I can do this!" but to my dismay the bar remains pretty flat. I think about winning $1,000,000, but don't get much of a jump for that either. Then I picture myself running with a cheering crowd and music playing, and the bar goes through the roof.

For the study, participants were placed in one of four groups. All four groups started out by getting in the scanner and trying to activate their brains using motivation strategies, but first without receiving any feedback. After doing this for several minutes, people in the first group (like me) would try again, but this time would see a thermometer on the computer screen in front of them. When activity in the VTA went up, the bar on the thermometer would rise. When activity in the VTA went down, the thermometer would drop. The other groups either got feedback from a different brain region, got fake feedback, or were shown a visual distraction. These groups were used as comparisons to ensure that it really was the signal from the VTA that was being registered in the neurofeedback group. Afterward, all four groups tried one more time without the feedback (real or fake). At the end of the study, all participants were debriefed about their group assignment and the purpose of the study.

The results were published recently in the journal *Neuron*. It turns out that the strategies people tried initially did not activate their VTAs very much–the same experience I had. In other words, what people thought of as motivating did not match up with activity in what we consider to be the "motivation center" of the brain. How could that be? One possible explanation is that it can be difficult to get a sense of just how motivated we are to do something. Consider times when you might have thought you were highly motivated ("I know I am going to stick to my diet/exercise regimen this year"), and didn't follow through. Another interpretation is that while we might have some sense of how motivated we are in a given moment, our subjective perceptions might not translate to VTA activation. There might not even be a clear feeling associated with the activation at all, explains MacInnes. That's where the feedback came in.

The study found that, like me, people were better able to activate their VTAs, on average, once they got neurofeedback compared to people who got false feedback or no feedback. And the learning stuck–once people knew the strategies that worked for them, they were effective even once the feedback was taken away. Overall, different strategies worked for different people and some people in the control groups were still able to activate their VTAs even without the neurofeedback. The take-home message is that there is still a lot to learn.

Perhaps the biggest unanswered question is what could result from an ability to better activate one's VTA. One possibility is that internally generated VTA activation could allow people to have the extra oomph to better meet their goals. So maybe when I need to do errands, but am really not in the mood, I can think about winning a race and it will give me the drive to go to the grocery store. For others, enhanced VTA activation might be able to help with studying. After all, studies have found VTA activation associated with better memory performance. And given other studies showing VTA signaling being related to eating and mood, it's possible that it could help people with eating disorders or depression. Time will tell whether this method will be useful clinically, but for now I can say for certain that it can be a lot of fun getting to know your brain–and for me at least, it seems that having fun is one of the keys to activating my VTA.

About the Author

Matthew Scult is a PhD candidate in the Department of Psychology and Neuroscience at Duke University. More about his research and writing can be found at www.matthewscult.com or follow him on Twitter @NeuroMatt1.

Pinpointing the Brain's Motivation Switch

By Leslie Nemo

Pinpointing where motivation resides in the brain is not easy, but a research team in China may have done just that. The group isolated a small group of neurons in the brains of mice that play a critical role in persistent behavior, according to a study published today in *Science*. This handful of brain cells is known as the dorsomedial prefrontal cortex, or dmPFC, and it sits in a region integral for learning appropriate social behavior. When the team fired up the neurons using light, the dmPFC motivated the mice to win competitions in which they had previously lacked the will to succeed. In other words, "this might provide a new biological basis for what people call 'grit,'" says Hailan Hu, a neuroscientist at Zhejiang University who led the research.

In the case of these mice, "grit" requires upsetting hierarchies. Male mice that live together establish and maintain social rankings, Hu explains. To figure out which mice were dominant, she and her colleagues released two mice at a time into a narrow tube, one at each end. To get out, one animal–the lower-ranked individual–had to back up whereas the other, higher-ranking individual had to push forward. Most studies of mouse social hierarchy have focused on more aggressive behaviors such as how male mice might pick on new cage members, says Helmut Kessels, a neurologist at the Netherlands Institute for Neuroscience who was not involved with the research. "In this case it's just four mice in a cage who live in peace," he says, which helps strengthen the team's argument that they were assessing motivation, not hostility.

In a previous study Hu's research team used neuron-disrupting molecules to prove the relationship between dmPFC activity and a mouse's decision to surrender to or push back against its cage mate in the tube task. But the technique they used for modifying the dmPFC's activity levels took between 12 and 24 hours to work. "It was relatively slow for us to see a very direct causal relationship," Hu says. This time around, she and her team wanted much more precise, instantaneous control of the brain region. So, they inserted a virus into the dmPFC that expresses a light-sensitive protein, along with a fiber-optic cable. When the team pulsed laser light through the wire, it instantly regulated the protein's expression, turning the neurons "on" or "off." With their prefrontal cortex switched "on" 80 to 90 percent of the treated mice pushed out opponents they had yielded to before the neural interventions.

When the mice were placed in the tube chambers without any kind of brain intervention, those that had behaved dominantly multiple times the day before kept their ranking. The team suspected the mice had undergone a kind of neural circuit workout–the repeated winning had perpetuated their drive to win. An earlier study had identified the connection between the thalamus–a brain region that relays incoming signals from the muscles and senses–and the dmPFC, along with the role this neural circuit can play in modifying a mouse's desire for confrontation. With that in mind, Hu and her team honed in on a region where the thalamus meets the dmPFC. Sure enough, activating that connection inspired the same drive to win. This detail of the research–showing this brain circuit can adapt to winning–is what really makes this study stand out, Kessels says.

The mice shifted on the scoreboard not because they were made bigger or stronger–the researchers paired up mice of similar sizes and measured no change in testosterone levels after the contests. Neither did the altered mice defend their territory and attack when new mice entered their cage, as they would if their aggression levels had risen, according to Hu. Mice adapted to winning showed their skills outside the tubes, too. When the team exposed cage mates to an ice-cold floor with one warm corner, the same social-climbing phenomena occurred. The newly dominant mice spent more time in the hot corner than they did when they were lower-ranking, even though their dmPFCs were no longer being artificially activated by

Hu and her team. The findings suggest the experiments were truly testing the mouse's drive to win.

Words like "drive" or "grit" sound like very human qualities, Hu says, but she thinks they are reasonable terms for translating the shift in mouse behavior to something humans can recognize. Kessels phrases the phenomena another way: The neurons of the winning mice have adapted to victory, he says, so they learn to expect a win. This trained anticipation could potentially help athletes or anyone in a competition, Hu notes. If you first face multiple opponents you easily beat, she says, you might be psychologically geared up to win again, even against a more challenging competitor.

About the Author

Leslie Nemo is a freelance science journalist living in Brooklyn, N.Y. You can find more of her work at www.leslienemo.com

Section 4: Self-Discipline

Why Feeling Close to the Finish Line Makes You Push Harder

By Katy Milkman and Kassie Brabaw

Everyone has goals they're striving to achieve, even during a global pandemic. Maybe you're a scientist working around the clock to find a cure for COVID-19 (if so, thank you and good luck!). Or maybe you're stuck working from home and pushing hard to hit 10,000 steps a day while confined to a small, urban living space. Whatever it is you're striving to achieve, science shows you're likely to push harder the closer you feel to the finish line. When researchers first speculated about this tendency, they called it the goal gradient hypothesis. And it turns out to have interesting implications not only for predicting when we'll push ourselves the hardest, but also for marketers hoping to convince us to buy our next cup of coffee or take our next airline flight (at least, once we start flying again).

Oleg Urminsky, a professor of marketing at the University of Chicago Booth School of Business, has been studying the goal gradient hypothesis since he was a doctoral student. Recently, Katy Milkman, a professor at the Wharton School of the University of Pennsylvania, got to chat with Urminsky in an interview for the podcast *Choiceology.*

[An edited transcript of the interview follows.]

Milkman: Can you explain what the goal gradient hypothesis is?

Urminsky: The basic idea is that the closer we get to completing a goal, the more motivated we are to continue working on it and achieve that goal.

Milkman: Can you please explain how your classic 2006 paper demonstrated this?

Urminsky: There were some early studies that tried to test this in a couple of ways. Two of my favorites: in one, some researchers designed an apparatus they would attach cigarettes to, bring smokers into the lab, and then the smoker would have to pull the cigarette on this sliding apparatus into their mouth to take a drag.

This was done in the 1970s. They tried to measure this idea that they'd pull faster as the cigarette was almost in their mouth. Of course, you probably don't want this cigarette-laden apparatus to crash into your face, so they didn't find any results there.

There was another study that looked at people going into a bank to cash checks and they tried to measure how fast they were walking. This highlights a difference between rats in a lab and humans, which is that we pace ourselves. You probably don't see people breaking into a run as they get to the door of a cafeteria. We know the reward is going to be there and we decide how much effort to put in and how quickly to walk for these kinds of rewards that are already certain to us.

We wanted to test our idea that, in humans, this goal gradient was more likely to apply conceptually when we're thinking about the different goals in our life and how to prioritize them, how much effort to put into each one at what time. We thought a good laboratory for this motivational difference was loyalty programs.

Think "buy 10, get one free" coffee programs, or airline frequent flyer miles. If you think about the coffee program: You're thirsty, you want to get something to drink, you could either go to the coffee shop downstairs where you have a loyalty card or you could go somewhere else. How you choose between those things might be affected by your trying to complete that coffee card. Our main study was in a buy 10, get one free coffee card program on campus. We managed this program, collected the cards, and measured how long it took people to come back for their next coffee as a function of how many stamps they already had on their card. When you have only one stamp on your card, nine to go, are you going to be less motivated, and therefore it'll take you longer to come back and buy another coffee, than if you already have eight stamps and only two left to go? That's exactly what we found.

Milkman: Why do you think it is that people behave this way?

Urminsky: I think the way basic cognition is organized prioritizes things that are larger rewards and rewards that we're closer to achieving. And in rats, that plays out in a very simple and direct way. But for humans, everything we do is filtered through much more complex, higher-order cognition.

Another way of saying it would be that we're present-biased, and that's actually part of what's going on. When you only have one stamp on your card, that's pretty far away. Whereas when you only have two stamps to go, that coffee is imminent–you could get it really soon. And so, it seems more valuable.

My guess is that we spontaneously think about goals more if they can be achieved sooner and that we also take them more seriously and value them more.

Milkman: I would love it if you could talk about the "progress illusion" and how it relates to the progress illusion.

Urminsky: There's a lot of research showing that humans try to form judgments and use heuristics to simplify complex decisions. What that suggests is that maybe it's not the actual distance to the goal that matters in human behavior, but our perception of that distance. And so, the progress illusion is theoretically interesting as a way to test if motivation is about real goal proximity or subjective perception.

The basic idea is to hold constant the objective distance to the goal, but make some people feel like the goal is pretty close and others feel like the goal is farther away. And so, in the study we designed two different kinds of these coffee cards. One was a 12-stamp card, but we started people off with two free stamps. The other version was a standard card, just buy 10 coffees, get one free.

In both cases when people get the card, they're 10 coffees away from receiving their reward. But in the first case, by framing it as 12 stamps and giving them two free stamps, they feel like they're already part of the way there.

People completed cards faster if they thought of it as the remaining 10 out of 12 as opposed to the full 10 required. You can see this in lots of different real-world settings. Plenty of rewards programs will give you free points to start.

Milkman: Where do you think this finding matters outside of the domain of rewards programs? Could this even be important for people who are trying to pursue goals?

Urminsky: One of my colleagues, Devin Pope, has a great study looking at standardized testing. He looks at a setting where there's different tests on different days and the students know in advance which subject will be administered first, second, third or fourth.

He finds that students consistently score higher on the first test. The idea is that the week before, they're sitting there thinking about these four goals that they're trying to achieve, which is to do well on four different tests covering four different topics, and they focus their efforts on the one that's the closest. They think of the first topic, "let me study really hard for that one." And they maybe overprioritize that first one.

This implies that understanding the goal gradient is important for managing our own motivation because it can be a double-edged sword. On the one hand, having a salient goal that we're committed to with a clear deadline or requirement is really motivating. It focuses our attention, gets us to muster our energy and really work on achieving that goal. It's a great source of motivation and we can use that by setting up our goals in a way that we always have a goal in our sights that feels close.

The potential dark side of the goal gradient is that when we're really focused on the proximal goal, it can make us shortsighted, just like the students. And so, the flip side of understanding the goal gradient is realizing that it can be really helpful to motivate us to have this upcoming goal in our sights, but we want to make sure it's not blinding us to other, later goals that are equally or maybe even more important.

Milkman: Is there anything you do differently in your life as a result of the research on this topic?

Urminsky: What I'd love to tell you is that I'm great at time management and at prioritizing projects and my work. Unfortunately, I'm the classic case of people studying what they're bad at because they find it fascinating.

I have a very long to-do list and I use goal setting to try to prioritize. And then I struggle with how a goal that's really in your face can distract us from longer-term, potentially more important goals. If I'm working on multiple projects and one of them is with a coauthor and I have a meeting with that coauthor the next day, that seems like the most important thing in the world, even if there's something else that's a lot more urgent but where the next step in completing that goal is less salient or less immediate.

Milkman: Have you found any cures for suffering from it? Do you do anything where you try to dodge it or do you have any sophisticated tips you can offer?

Urminsky: The strategy I'd recommend, although I haven't tested it scientifically–I've tried to test it in my personal life with mixed results–is to do goal prioritization with a bit of a colder mindset, where you're thinking of *all* your goals as a little bit distant and trying to be objective about how important they are. And then, take the most important goals and put them first on your list and think of ways to make those goals feel immediate.

We all have this intuition of knowing that this is helpful even if we don't know why. For goals that are really far off, try to break them up into pieces and focus on the part that you can complete soon to make progress on that motivating. And so, if I'm writing a paper, thinking about the fact that, in the best case, it's going to be published two years from now, might be demotivating.

But if, instead, I pick a day by which I want to have the first draft done, I'm going to reframe it in my head and feel more motivated.

About the Author

Katy Milkman is a behavioral scientist and James G. Dinan Professor of Operations, Information and Decisions at the Wharton School at the University of Pennsylvania. She is also author of the book How to Change: The Science of Getting from Where You Are to Where You Want to Be, *host of the podcast Choiceology and co-director of the Behavior Change for Good Initiative. Follow Milkman on Twitter @Katy_Milkman.*

Having a "Plan B" Can Hurt Your Chances of Success

By Katherine Milkman and Jihae Shin

Imagine two aspiring entrepreneurs: Meg and Jen. They are equally capable and well-connected, and they are working on equally promising startup ideas. In fact, imagine that Meg and Jen differ in just one respect: Meg is *thinking* about what a good fallback job would be and how she plans to pursue it if her current startup fails while Jen is not.

Who do you think will work harder and in turn, have a better chance of success: Meg or Jen? Might merely thinking through a backup plan be enough to undermine Meg's motivation and likelihood of success?

This was the question that we wanted to answer with our research. And yes, we find in a paper published in *Organizational Behavior and Human Decision Processes* that merely contemplating a backup plan can reduce the effort you put forth to achieve a goal, thus hurting your chances of achieving it. Most people think that making a backup plan is always a good idea, and previous scholarship has focused almost exclusively on the benefits of planning. However, we highlight an unintended cost of making backup plans: a lower chance of successfully achieving your primary goal.

We started our investigation with a simple survey at a large east-coast train station. Our research assistants approached people who were waiting for trains. We asked them to write about a goal they were pursuing and how much effort they were putting forth towards achieving their goal. Then, participants were asked if they had made a backup plan for their goal. Analyzing the data, we found that the people who had made a backup plan were putting forth less effort towards achieving their goals. Although this finding was consistent with our hunch about the risks of making backup plans, correlation does not equal causation. It's possible that people who were working less hard towards their goal were more likely to make a backup plan because they knew they were more likely to need one. Or maybe, people who didn't really care much about goal achievement to begin with were putting in less effort and were more likely to make a backup plan.

We wanted to find out whether the observed relationship between making a backup plan and effort was indeed casual: did thinking through a backup plan make people put forth less effort towards their goals, ultimately leading to lower chances of success? In one experiment, we brought undergraduates into a room and gave them the task of unscrambling scrambled words into sentences. We promised them an energy bar as a reward for high performance. We randomly assigned a prompt to half of these people that encouraged them to think through a backup plan to put in place in case they failed to get a free snack: we asked them to think of other ways they could find free food on campus in case they didn't earn the free snack in our study. Sure enough, we found those who made backup plans before starting the task didn't perform as well in the task. In subsequent experiments, we replicated our findings in other contexts with different rewards (e.g., money, saved time) and confirmed that this effect was not driven by mundane factors like being tired out from generating backup plans, or viewing the reward as less valuable.

So we'd found this robust effect, but we still wanted to find out why it was happening. Is making a backup plan reducing motivation or is it a source of distraction? In our final study, we dug into this question and found that people who thought through backup plans before working towards the goal in our study wanted the proffered rewards less intensely than others. So this suggests that thinking through a backup plan actually makes you want to achieve your primary goal less, which then hurts your effort, performance, and ultimately, your chances of successfully achieving your goal.

Fascinating, right? And probably disheartening to some! Now the question becomes, what do you do with this information? How can this research help you make better decisions, and at the same time still let you plan wisely when pursuing goals that you can't be certain you'll achieve?

First of all, it's important to know that these results do not apply to all goals–they only apply to goals whose success is highly dependent on effort. Since we find that the negative effect of making a backup plan is reduced motivation and effort towards a goal, making a backup plan would not harm success on goals where success is not contingent on effort (e.g., winning the lottery). So feel free to make a backup plan without hesitation for how you'll support yourself if you don't strike it rich in Powerball!

Second, you may not have to choose between 'making a backup plan now' and 'not making one ever'; it may be a question of *when* you make a backup plan. For example, you might want to consider making a backup plan after you have done everything you can to achieve your primary goal. In other words, consider making a backup plan after your goal-related efforts wrap up and the outcome is now in someone else's hand (e.g., your coworker's, a judge's, etc.). If you are an entrepreneur, you might want to consider committing to one startup idea for a certain period of time, devoting your energy and attention to that one project during that timeframe, and then committing to start thinking about backup plans if and only if things haven't worked out by your deadline. This same strategy could also apply when you are trying to get your dream job or applying to schools.

Third, if you manage multiple people or teams at work, you might want to assign the task of pursuing a certain goal (i.e., getting a product launched) to one person or team and the task of making a backup plan in case of goal failure to someone else. You might even want to consider making it a secret that someone else is thinking through backup plans. That way, you may be able to protect the motivation and performance of the people who are actively pursuing your organization's primary goals while still managing risk and mitigating uncertainty.

Many of the goals we pursue in life require a great deal of effort, and we can't be certain of achieving them. The insurance of having a backup plan is thus very attractive. However, this psychological insurance, just like other insurances, may come with a price.

About the Author

Katherine Milkman is an Associate Professor of Operations, Information and Decisions at The Wharton School of the University of Pennsylvania and the co-director of the Wharton People Analytics Initiative.

Jihae Shin is an Assistant Professor of Management and Human Resources at The Wisconsin School of Business of the University of Wisconsin-Madison.

Need More Self-Control? Try a Simple Ritual

By Francesca Gino

Many of our most vexing problems, from overeating to not saving enough for retirement to not working out enough have something in common: lack of self-control. Self-control is what gives us the capacity to say no to choices that are immediately gratifying but costly in the long term—that piece of chocolate cake (instead of an apple), that afternoon in front of the couch (instead of a visit to the gym). Despite our best intentions, we often fail to meet our lofty goals.

The problem of self-control has puzzled psychologists and behavioral scientists for decades. A great deal of research has identified situations in which self-control failures are likely to happen and tools to help people exercise better control. For instance, research has found that people persist for longer on tasks that require self-control when they know they'll be paid for their efforts, or when they are told that their work will benefit others (such as helping find a cure for Alzheimer's disease). These motivating incentives can increase our self-control, at least up to a point.

Entrepreneurs have also become interested in self-control, as is evident from the many diet and exercise apps and gadgets on the market. To take one notable example, on the commitment contract website stickK.com, users put down some money (say, $200) and state a goal they want to achieve (such as to lose ten pounds in a month). They also need to state what will happen to the money if they don't stick to their commitments (eg, it'll go to a friend or to a charity they do not like). If they meet their goal, they earn their money back. If they don't, they lose the money.

Tools like stickK.com can be effective, but they are often difficult to implement; you may need to enlist someone to help monitor your efforts. New research my colleagues and I conducted point to a different solution that may be easier to implement: using rituals.

A ritual is a series of steps we take while attaching some kind of symbolic meaning. Players in all sorts of sports have rituals that involve actions such as eating the same foods in exactly the same order before a game or listening to the same pre-ordered playlist a given number of times. From the way some prepare their coffee to the way people celebrate important life events, like weddings or graduations, rituals are a part of our daily life. And though they may seem useless, or even silly, research has found that rituals are powerful.

In the past, my colleagues and I have found that rituals reduce anxiety before stressful tasks, and improve performance. They allow us to enjoy our family holidays more. And they also give us a greater sense of control after experiencing a loss, whether a loved one or in a lottery. Given the power of rituals, we thought we might test their effectiveness in resisting temptation.

In one study, we tested the power of rituals to help with a common self-control problem: eating less. We visited a university gym and recruited undergraduate females who already had a goal of losing weight. We told half of them to be mindful about their food consumption for the next five days. We taught the other half a three-step pre-eating ritual and told them to complete it every time they ate something. The ritual, which we created rather randomly, did not require participants to eat less food and did not directly interfere with consumption. Here's the ritual:

> First, cut your food into pieces before you eat it. Second, rearrange the pieces so that they are perfectly symmetric on your plate. That is, get the right half of your plate to look exactly the same as the left half of your plate. Finally, press your eating utensil against the top of your food three times. In order to be in the study, you must do the three steps of this ritual each time you eat.

To track daily food and beverage intake, we asked participant to download the "MyFitnessPal" food-tracking app onto their phone. MyFitnessPal allows users to list exactly the type and amount of food or beverage they consume, including brands of grocery products and meals from chain restaurants. Three times per day, participants' phones would remind them to log their food intake, and the experimenter had access to these online food diaries.

As we expected, participants who enacted the pre-eating ritual consumed fewer calories (about 1,424 calories for each day, on average) as compared to those who simply were mindful about their eating (who consumed about 1,648). Those who performed the ritual also ate less fat and less sugar. The ritual helped them exercise the self-control needed to achieve their weight loss goals. Interestingly, at the end of the study, our participants said they thought the ritual was not very helpful and reported they were unlikely to continue it.

In another study, we examined whether simple rituals could also help people make healthier choices when tempted with unhealthy ones. We invited college students to the laboratory and told them they would complete a taste test of carrots and chocolate. They received four bags from the experimenter: three that each contained one baby carrot, and a fourth that contained a Lindt chocolate truffle.

We divided participants in three groups: those engaging in a ritual, those making random gestures (all polite ones!), and those who simply ate carrots (our control condition). Those in our ritual condition were given a series of steps to perform before eating each carrot:

1. Make a fist with your right hand. Using your knuckles, knock on the table twice.
2. Now, take out the first [second] [third] plastic bag and put it in front of you.
3. Then, use your right hand and knock twice again on the table.
4. Now, take a deep breath and close your eyes for two seconds.

Before they ate the third carrot, they answered two questions about eating the third carrot and finally learned they had a choice between eating the third carrot or a chocolate.

Those in our random-gestures condition completed a different set of steps before eating each carrot; they too were given a choice between eating the carrot (the healthy option) or the chocolate (the tempting, unhealthy one).

In the third subgroup (the control condition), participants simply ate the first two carrots, answered the same two questions, and were given the final choice without performing any additional steps.

About 58 percent of the participants in our ritual condition chose the carrot over the chocolate, as compared to only about 35 percent of those in the control condition and 46 percent of those in the random-gestures condition. Thus, participants who enacted a ritual while eating carrots subsequently made healthier choices as compared to those in the other groups. The results suggest that following a stringent set of steps, however strange, before eating may be a better weight-loss strategy than adhering to a stringent diet.

It is important to note that rituals like the ones we created and used in our research can be taken too far. When a repeated set of actions that restrict food consumption start to become mindlessly followed, as by habit, they can lead to problematic behaviors such as eating disorders, research finds. But undertaken conscientiously and carefully, such practices can also promote well-being.

Psychology research has found that our behaviors lead us to conclusions about ourselves: donating money to the homeless causes us to view ourselves as caring, and giving up our seat on the subway leads us to believe we're polite, for instance. Following a series of steps over and over again, which happens when we use rituals, requires some good self-discipline. So, we reasoned, when we see ourselves engaging in a ritual, we code that behavior as a sign that we are people with self-control. And thanks to that self-control, we choose the apple (or carrot) over the chocolate and thus reduce our caloric intake.

Classical Confucian philosophy places a lot of emphasis on ritual. It may be no surprise, then, that evidence suggests that East Asians from highly ritualized Confucian cultures have stronger self-regulation skills than people from Western cultures. Likewise, the military lifestyle across cultures is known to induce both self-discipline and behavioral regulation, perhaps in part due to its many rituals, including marching, chanting and other regimented behaviors that ensure order and high levels of motivation. At the outset, these rituals may seem like a waste of time. Yet, as our research suggests, they are quite powerful. Even when they are not embedded in years of tradition, simple rituals can help us build personal discipline and self-control. With a simple ritual, that piece of chocolate cake may not look as tempting.

About the Author

Francesca Gino is an award-winning behavioral scientist and Tandon Family Professor of Business Administration at Harvard Business School. She is author of Rebel Talent: Why It Pays to Break the Rules at Work and in Life, *as well as* Sidetracked: Why Our Decisions Get Derailed, and How We Can Stick to the Plan. *Follow her on Twitter @francescagino.*

A Self-Improvement Secret: Work on Strengths

By Lauren Howe

How would you like to improve yourself? We've probably all paused to ask ourselves this question (perhaps around New Year's). Maybe you aimed to start exercising or stop procrastinating. Or was it losing weight? Or working on a case of low self-esteem?

These are the goals people often list in online forums about self-improvement, and they share a common thread. When considering what they'd like to improve about themselves, people jump straight to weaknesses. If you ask people how they decide what to target, they say, "I look at what makes me unhappy or what I'm unsatisfied with," or "I think about the areas of my life in which I've been struggling." To improve, it's said you should *become aware of your bad habits* and *focus on recognizing your faults*.

But why give so much attention to improving our weaknesses? Why not build on our strengths?

New research by psychologists Andreas Steimer and André Mata sheds light on these questions. The team found that people believe that they can change their weaknesses more than their strengths. In one study, people listed a personality trait that they saw as a central strength (something that they really liked about themselves). They also listed a personality trait that they saw as a central weakness (something that they really disliked about themselves). Then, these people answered questions about how changeable these traits are. For instance, they answered how much they agreed that this trait "is a part of me that I cannot change very much." The results showed that people thought they would be able to work on their weaknesses more than their strengths.

Of course, a first step to self-improvement is often thinking about what you can control. Just think of how the Serenity Prayer (made famous by Alcoholics Anonymous) asks for the wisdom to know the difference between what we can and cannot change. Believing that weaknesses are more changeable then strengths could lead us down this path of choosing to tackle our weaknesses when it comes to self-improvement. And there are obvious positives to believing that weaknesses can change, like inspiring a commitment to self-improvement.

This could have its downsides, though. We might end up wasting our time trying to get rid of a bad habit. Despite our best intentions, New Year's resolutions often fail. These resolutions target weaknesses that are really hard to change. Psychologists who study "false hope syndrome" find that people are overconfident in their ability to change, and this leads people to set unrealistic goals for themselves. Someone might decide that they want to become more studious, and vow to spend every Friday night in the library. When they are tempted to go to a friend's birthday party one Friday night instead, they may throw in the towel and give up on their goal entirely. If they'd set more reasonable goals (for example, to study one extra hour per week), they might have been able to stick with their plan for self-improvement. In fact, the researchers who conducted the study on beliefs about strengths and weaknesses found the further away someone was from who they wanted to be, the more they believed they could change themselves to become like this ideal person. Could the belief that weaknesses are changeable lead people to set unrealistic goals?

Even more interestingly: what opportunities might we miss out on if we simply accept the existence of our strengths? Neglecting the *practice* of strengths – failing to work on the good things that we already have – could overlook a source of happiness. In fact, programs designed to "train your strengths" can have benefits.

Some researchers have tested programs called "positive interventions" that give people the chance to uncover, explore, and practice their strengths. In one such program, people take a test to identify their top five character strengths, and then are tasked with using these strengths in a new and different way every day for a week. Researchers found that people who practiced their strengths in this way were happier and less depressed six months later.

Neglecting strengths might also have negative consequences. People may believe that their weaknesses will be lost over time, but that their strengths are there to stay. Because of this, we might not be very motivated to work on our strengths. Imagine a person who feels that they are a particularly kind person, and that this will never change. She or he might not take the time to cultivate kindness even further – for instance, to go out of her or his way to volunteer or help other people. Perhaps this person would instead let these habits slide, and – secure in her or his "kindness" – would actually become less kind over time. If we don't actively engage with our strengths, we might see them fade.

So what can we do? Luckily, research shows that our beliefs about what we can and cannot change can *themselves* be changed. Changing these beliefs shapes how people deal with all sorts of setbacks in their lives, from low grades to breakups, and also shapes people's goals. For example, if people believe that intelligence can be developed, they take on more challenging problems to improve their intelligence. If we choose to think about our ability to develop our strengths, we might seek out different opportunities for self-growth that capitalize on our strengths. One way to improve yourself is to sharpen a skill you already have.

About the Author

Lauren Howe is a doctoral candidate in Social Psychology at Stanford University. She received her BA from the University of Virginia in 2010 and completed a Fulbright English Teaching Assistantship in Reutlingen, Germany. You can follow her on Twitter @howelaurenc.

How to Avoid the Temptations of Immediate Gratification

By Melanie Bauer

Happy New Year! It's 2013 and you've vowed to cut sweets out of your diet. Despite your desire for a trimmer body, the sight of cupcakes in a café window overpowers your good intentions. You cannot resist the small, sweet reward even though the larger, delayed reward of a healthier body is ultimately more desirable.

What leads some of us to give in to our immediate urges, while others are able to endure the wait for bigger and better outcomes? Neuroeconomists are investigating the brain to answer this question. They are interested in comparing the brain activity of individuals who act impulsively–those who choose rewards now over later–to that of patient folks.

Traditionally, the assumption of researchers in this field, and the related field of behavioral economics, has been that impulsive people choose immediate rewards simply because they dislike waiting. In these prior studies, when presented with a hypothetical choice between, say, \$50 now or \$100 in a year, impulsive individuals went for the \$50. Additionally, they showed a greater brain response to the immediate \$50 reward–in the part of the brain that represents how much you are enjoying a reward (the ventral striatum)–than did patient people. Researchers interpreted this brain response as the impulsive individuals' preference for immediacy. So while impulsive individuals would claim "carpe diem" and "strike while the iron is hot" as their life mantras, the less quoted "carpent tua poma nepotes" and "good things come to those who wait" are patient individuals' words to live by.

However, impulsivity may not simply be due to how long people are willing to wait for gratification. A recent study by a team of researchers at Washington University in St. Louis found that when people waited for a reward, patient people were seen–through the lens of a functional magnetic resonance imaging (fMRI) machine–imagining the future. In more patient people, the researchers observed increased activity in the region of the brain that helps you think about the future (the anterior prefrontal cortex). The patient individuals, it seems, devoted more energy to imagining receiving their reward later.

What sets this Washington University study apart from previous studies is that researchers have never before focused on the brain responses of individuals after they make a decision and are waiting for their reward. Instead, researchers have typically measured brain activity while people are making their choices. Prior researchers likely disregarded the waiting period because their studies used hypothetical rewards over long delays. Because people weren't actually waiting in real time to receive a real reward, the researchers could not monitor the brain during this waiting period. This new study presented people with real rewards in the form of squirts of juice either immediately or at a delay of up to a minute. In fact, the researchers squirted the juice straight into the mouths of study subjects, in much the same way that animals have been rewarded in similar studies.

This future thinking, which is associated with the anterior prefrontal cortex (aPFC), has also been found in neuropsychological studies that focus on two different, but related phenomena: prospective memory–remembering to do something in the future, like fill up your gas tank on the way home from work–and episodic future thought–thinking about the future, such as imagining what you'll cook for dinner later tonight. Now, one more phenomenon can be added to the list of contexts in which people imagine a future outcome and activate their aPFC: imagining future rewards.

One problem with the future is its vagueness. While you are able to imagine in your mind going to the gas station or cooking dinner in general, the exact details of these activities are not clear. You don't know which pump you'll use at the gas station, or precisely what time you'll remove the pizza from the oven. In this way, the future is fuzzy. This fuzziness can make the future less appealing.

Remember the marshmallow experiment that tested the willpower of children to resist the temptation to eat a marshmallow placed on a table in front of them, so they could receive two marshmallows after they waited? Research suggests that if that one marshmallow was made more abstract–such as hiding it from view or just showing a picture of it–the reward would become less appealing and more similar in appeal to receiving two marshmallows at a future time. On the flip side, making the future less fuzzy by focusing on the details–eating double the marshmallows currently being presented–could also make the future marshmallows more attractive than the present singular marshmallow. In this way kids would have an easier time resisting the one marshmallow now in exchange for the two marshmallows in the future.

Perhaps a combination of this fuzziness research (i.e., delay of gratification research) with recent neuroeconomics research–linking impulsivity with a lack of future thinking–could be useful for clinicians who are developing treatment plans for impulsive individuals. Because the future is fuzzy and impulsive people have an especially hard time imagining it, clinical treatments could involve de-emphasizing the present, making it more abstract, and building a concrete image of the future. For example, while it may be quicker, easier, and cheaper to buy fast food for dinner–immediate rewards that are all very desirable–people could learn to visualize larger future rewards when deciding what to eat, such as avoiding ailments like obesity and Type-2 diabetes. They could also avoid driving past their favorite fast food restaurants and only stock their cupboards with nutritious foods so the most visually salient meal options are healthy ones. This could help shift the attractive light from being cast on the present desire for fast food to instead being on the future desire for a healthy body.

For impulsive individuals who repeatedly make decisions that satisfy their current desires at the expense of their future needs, the negative effects on their health can be significant. Given the host of public health issues that involve impulsivity, research in neuroeconomics could prove important. Future research could measure the effects of an intervention on the brain. Can we get impulsive people to produce activity in their brain that shows they're thinking about the future in a concrete way, making them look and act more patiently in the laboratory? Do these interventions lead to real-life choices to invest in the future and not give in to present impulses? Not to mention, could adapting the mindset that the future is worth waiting for help the rest of us keep some of our New Year's resolutions?

About the Author

Melanie Bauer is a graduate student in psychology at Washington University in St. Louis studying cognitive aging. She will write her dissertation on informal science education, and has also contributed to The Open Notebook. *Connect with Melanie on Twitter @MelanieSBauer.*

Section 5: The Habits of Addiction and Compulsion

Disrupting the Habits of Anorexia

By Deborah R. Glasofer and Joanna Steinglass

Every day on the dot of noon, Jane* would eat her 150-calorie lunch: nonfat yogurt and a handful of berries. To eat earlier, she felt, would be "gluttonous." To eat later would disrupt the dinner ritual. Jane's eating initially became more restrictive in adolescence, when she worried about the changes her body was undergoing in the natural course of puberty. When she first settled on her lunchtime foods and routine–using a child-size spoon to "make the yogurt last" and sipping water between each bite–she felt accomplished. Jane enjoyed her friends' compliments about her "incredible willpower." In behavioral science terms, her actions were goal-directed, motivated by achieving a particular outcome. In relatively short order, she got the result she really wanted: weight loss.

Years later Jane, now in her 30s and a newspaper reporter, continued to eat the same lunch in the same way. Huddled over her desk in the newsroom, she tried to avoid unwanted attention and feared anything that might interfere with the routine. She no longer felt proud of her behavior. Her friends stopped complimenting her "self-control" years ago, when her weight plummeted perilously low. So low that she has had to be hospitalized on more than one occasion.

The longed-for weight loss did not make her feel better about herself or her appearance. Jane's curly hair, once shiny and thick, dulled and thinned; her skin and eyes lost their brightness. There were other costs as well–to her relationships, to her career. Instead of dreaming about a great romance, Jane would dream of the cupcakes she could not let herself have at her niece's birthday party. Instead of thinking about the best lead for her next story, she obsessed over calories and exercise.

Jane's ritualized and restrictive approach to food, her obsession with calories and her painfully low body weight are common symptoms of anorexia nervosa, a dangerous eating disorder that affects roughly one in 200 American women. Anorexia has a high relapse rate and ranks among the deadliest of all psychiatric conditions. Individuals with the disorder, about 10 percent of whom are men, enter a state of starvation that can cause numerous medical complications, including heart ailments, anemia, bone loss, infertility, and more. A young woman with this illness faces six times the average risk of death for someone her age, according to a 2011 meta-analysis of 36 studies, and mortality rises by 5 percent for every decade of illness.

Anorexia nervosa is often misunderstood by a public that tends to glorify thinness and view rule-ridden eating as an act of enviable self-control. This is nothing new. In the Middle Ages, a handful of religious figures, including Saint Catherine of Siena, were admired for engaging in extreme self-starvation—a condition termed "holy anorexia." Today we see self-starvation in the name of a culturally sanctioned pursuit of thinness. But there is nothing glorious about this disease, nor does it provide any actual measure of true control. Rigid, behavioral routines gradually close in on the afflicted individual until life becomes entirely about numbers on a food label, or a scale, or a clothing tag.

A new line of research suggests that the core of Jane's condition—her low weight—is not simply a matter of self-control. Rather her routines now occur almost automatically without regard for the outcome. Jane weighs herself each morning before she showers and again before she leaves for work. At each meal, she reads and rereads food labels for their nutritional breakdown. She cuts food into tiny pieces without thinking. In behavioral science terms, her mind has been overtaken by habit.

Habits can be incredibly useful. They allow the mind to multitask and in so doing enable efficiency. Behaviors get linked together into a routine, and once the chain of action is initiated, the rest follows with little mental effort. Yet sometimes habits take hold when they are not useful. We and others in the field are learning that this may occur with anorexia nervosa.

The habit-based model of the disorder offers a compelling explanation for why patients such as Jane struggle for years through chapters of outpatient and inpatient treatment without finding lasting recovery. If her illness is even partially explained by hijacked habit learning, it suggests that habit-busting techniques could be part of the solution. Habit-reversal therapy, for example, is well supported for conditions such as trichotillomania (hair-pulling disorder) and tic disorders. This type of treatment helps people become more aware of the cues that set their habits in motion and develop competing responses. For example, those with an urge to pull hair might be instructed to occupy their hands by imagining they are squeezing a lemon. We have adapted this approach for patients with anorexia in an intervention called REACH (*r*egulating *e*motions *a*nd *c*hanging *h*abits).

Jane worked with us in the REACH framework. The habit hypothesis made sense to her and helped her to feel better about why she had been stuck in routines that she knew were not healthy. We shared with her results from a brain-imaging study, published last year in *Nature Neuroscience*, that one of us (Steinglass) co-authored. It showed that when people with anorexia nervosa make decisions about what to eat, they use a different part of the brain—the dorsal striatum—than those without eating disorders. Studies in both animals and humans have shown that this deep-brain structure is involved with many aspects of behavior, one of which is habitual behavior.

In individual psychotherapy sessions, we helped Jane identify a number of habits that served the eating disorder better than they served her. At home and work she kept track of these routines and paid attention to their earliest cues. For example, Jane noticed that her mealtime rituals began with washing her hands. In therapy, she identified another action to try when faced with this cue. She began to bypass the sink, altering her route to the dining table. This small change made a difference in the subsequent chain of behaviors. Jane practiced moving her water glass out of arm's reach at the start of a meal; with improved awareness, it became easier to resist taking sips between each bite. Behaviorists refer to this as stimulus control: altering the environment to encourage an alternative behavior. In other instances, Jane developed competing responses—simple, motor-based counteractions–that made it harder to act out of habit. For example, she practiced picking up her utensils with her nondominant hand to help her take bigger and less "perfect" bites.

As new behaviors helped her break old habits, Jane tackled other routines of illness. For years she had kept a written record of what she ate at every meal. Jane decided to switch the location of her food journal, putting it out of her line of sight after meals. Instead of reaching for the journal, she turned to friends and family after eating–by phone or e-mail or in person if possible–which also provided an element of distraction. Nevertheless, this change provoked anxiety. To manage it, her therapist taught her a muscle-relaxation exercise–tensing one muscle at a time and then letting it go.

Most important, Jane learned that reversing or replacing old habits brought good outcomes. This was an essential element because behaviors that are associated with reinforcement grow stronger over time. During meals, Jane felt more present, and she found, to her pleasure, that she could participate more fully in conversation during and after eating. As she spent less time logging calories in her journal, she could focus instead on reading for work and leisure. Breaking these routines felt frightening at first, but loosening the grip of old preoccupations also brought an unanticipated element of relief. Jane's weight slowly improved, and although this change felt scary, she described feeling more motivated and able to maintain her new behaviors because they led to clearly positive rewards.

Encouraged by success with our initial patients, we have begun a small, randomized controlled trial to compare our habit-breaking approach with routine treatment for anorexia nervosa. By linking treatment directly with mechanisms of illness–in this case, the neural circuitry of habit–we hope to better understand this puzzling disorder, improve treatment and free more patients like Jane from the prison of habit.

**Jane is a pseudonym. Some details of her story have been altered to further protect her identity.*

Referenced

The Enigmatic Persistence of Anorexia Nervosa. B. Timothy Walsh in *American Journal of Psychiatry*, Vol. 170, No. 5, pages 477–484; May 2013.

Neural Mechanisms Supporting Maladaptive Food Choices in Anorexia Nervosa. Karin Foerde et al. in *Nature Neuroscience*, Vol. 18, pages 1571–1573; November 2015.

NeuroPod, *Nature*'s neuroscience podcast, on eating disorders: www.nature.com/neurosci/neuropod/index-2015-10-29.html

About the Authors

Deborah R. Glasofer, Ph.D., is an assistant professor of clinical psychology (in psychiatry) at the Columbia Center for Eating Disorders at the New York State Psychiatric Institute and at Columbia University Medical Center.

Joanna Steinglass, M.D., is an associate professor of clinical psychiatry at the Columbia Center for Eating Disorders at the New York State Psychiatric Institute and at Columbia University Medical Center.

Enhancing the Brain's Flexibility Could Unseat Addiction

By Michele Solis

Reid had been drinking hard since 1994, when sickness, his father's death and business troubles had him reaching for more alcohol than usual. Eventually he was knocking back 10 or more drinks a day. In 2009 his family leveled an ultimatum. He had to give up alcohol or get out.

"That choice sounds real simple, but it's very, very hard," says the 58-year-old college-educated businessman, whose last name has been withheld. "I've got a wife to die for and two of the greatest kids in the world, and I'm sitting there looking in the mirror, asking myself, 'You're going to give all this up for that drink?'" he remembers. Still, he drank, secretly downing miniature bottles of vodka while walking the dog, hiding out in the bathroom or going through the car wash.

An alcoholic's sense of being trapped in old habits reflects an underlying resistance to learning that scientists are now documenting at the molecular level. Over the past five years researchers have turned up evidence that using drugs and alcohol causes a loss of flexibility in the brain, including in the regions needed for changing habits. Even brief periods of drug use damage the junctions between neurons, known as synapses. Their healthy operation is critical to translating will into action. The very structures needed to dig a person out of addiction are eroded by drug use.

Researchers are now looking for ways to replenish this flexibility with compounds that adjust how the neurotransmitter glutamate, a chemical messenger in the brain, operates at the synapses. "We're trying to restore the brain machinery that allows a person to regain more control over their behavior," says Peter W. Kalivas, a professor at the Medical University of South Carolina, who studies the role of glutamate in addiction.

Returning the brain to a state where it is open to change, rather than resistant to it, could kick-start recovery. "This is not going to cure addiction, but it's definitely going to help," says Nora D. Volkow, director of the National Institute on Drug Abuse.

Drug-Induced Learning Problems

In the past scientists had focused primarily on how drugs take hold of the brain's reward regions. The new research on glutamate seeks to explain not how addiction sets in but why it is so hard to beat.

Even when addicts desperately want to stop, for fear of losing a job, a spouse or their life, they often still persist in taking drugs. Experts suspect this disconnect happens because drug use impairs a person's capacity to learn. Although scientists have long known that drug use induces a variety of cognitive shortcomings, during the past 10 years the learning deficit has emerged as a key reason why addicts stay addicted. In particular, addicts struggle to break old habits—even those not related to drug use.

This difficulty with developing a new routine can be measured in laboratory tests of "reversal learning" that ask a person to change how he or she responds to a familiar prompt. Addicts can learn an initial rule perfectly well, but they run into trouble when the rules change. In a 2006 study, for example, cocaine and alcohol abusers were asked to press a key each time they saw a green rectangle on a screen. After 500 repetitions, the rules changed so that the green rectangle signaled they were *not* to press the key. Healthy control participants soon withheld their key presses, but the addicts kept on pressing. Even when given feedback about their mistaken key pressing in a follow-up study, addicts still stuck with the old responses.

Addiction itself can be viewed as impaired reversal learning, says David Jentsch, a neuroscientist at the University of California, Los Angeles. A person first learns the rule: "When I use drugs, I feel good." Over time, as negative consequences accumulate, the rule changes to: "When I use drugs, bad things happen." "They know the new rule, they know things are getting bad, they know the drug isn't as positive as it once was," Jentsch says. "But they're unable to update their behavior." Reid, for instance, would convince himself that he could handle just one drink, despite plentiful evidence to the contrary. "I'd think one beer won't hurt, but next thing you know, I'd have blacked out," he says.

Animal studies indicate that this inability to update is a result of drug use rather than, say, an inherent trait of those likely to try drugs. In 2002 Jentsch and his colleagues reported that daily injections of cocaine for two weeks impaired reversal learning in vervet monkeys. Nine days after the last injection, monkeys learned by trial and error which of three objects hid a food treat underneath it. Once they figured it out, the food was hidden underneath a different object, and the monkeys had to discover the new location. Cocaine-naive monkeys readily adapted their choices, but cocaine-treated monkeys did not, continuing to select the object that had first hidden the food. Similar effects have since been found in rats and mice for cocaine, methamphetamine and alcohol.

Strung-Out Circuitry

Impairments in reversal learning reflect a brain working on automatic pilot. Behaviors ingrained as habits—whether looking in the same place for food or taking drugs—begin largely subconsciously until some surprise or consequence necessitates a change. The plan to change is then hatched in the brain's supervisory regions, within the prefrontal cortex, and implemented through that area's connections to regions that drive habitual behaviors, such as the nucleus accumbens, a sugar cube–size area buried underneath the cortex. "It's a self-control circuit," Jentsch says. "Think of it as where knowing meets doing."

These areas communicate by way of the synapses between neurons. To send a message, a neuron in the prefrontal cortex releases glutamate onto the receiving end of a neuron in the nucleus accumbens. There the glutamate molecules bind to proteins on the cell called receptors, like keys fitting into locks. The receptors then trigger a discharge of electricity from the neuron in the nucleus accumbens, which releases more neurotransmitters through its synapses, and the message is passed on. Strong synapses translate this glutamate message into a big electrical signal, whereas weak synapses convey only blips.

Researchers are finding that these synapses are unusually rigid in addiction, as though the nucleus accumbens receives the messages from the prefrontal cortex but cannot heed the instructions. Normally a synapse's strength varies over time, depending on the pattern of previous messages sent through it. For example, the rapid-fire release of glutamate leads to long-lasting boosts in electrical output. Yet in animals exposed to cocaine, no matter how much glutamate is released or how quickly it floods the synapse, the receptors trigger the same amount of electrical activity. Similar disruptions in synaptic plasticity are also found in animals exposed to methamphetamine, nicotine and heroin.

Kalivas and Volkow propose that this loss of flexibility prevents addicts from fully using information coming from the prefrontal cortex to curb their drug habits. "It's not like the connections have been burned out completely," Kalivas says about the lost flexibility at these synapses. "It's more subtle than that, which gives us hope we can fix it."

Refurbishing Synapses

Armed with the knowledge that restoring these synapses to their original, malleable state might help addicts, researchers began trying to figure out exactly which parts of the synapse are broken by addiction. Although a synapse is only a tiny point of contact between two neurons, it relies on a vast array of molecular machinery responsible for releasing and detecting glutamate messages.

The latest research suggests that several of these synaptic components are damaged by addiction. For example, in 2003 Kalivas's team found that cocaine decreases the amount of glutamate floating outside the neurons in the nucleus accumbens, in the space that surrounds brain cells and their tiny synapses. The lack of this signaling chemical ultimately distorts the glutamate messages sent through synapses by the prefrontal cortex.

Cocaine appears to cause this deficiency by reducing the number of glutamate-supplying protein pumps located on nearby support cells called glia. These pumps work by importing an amino acid called cysteine from the extracellular space and exporting glutamate into that space. Kalivas and other researchers wondered if supplying more cysteine to the brain could bump up the glutamate supply. They turned to a common compound used to treat a Tylenol (acetaminophen) overdose and included as a mucus buster in some cough syrups. In 2009 Kalivas showed in rats that this compound, called N-acetylcysteine (NAC), spurred the brain's remaining glutamate pumps into overdrive and returned glutamate levels to normal, restoring plasticity to the synapses.

In 2011 Kalivas's group linked this NAC-induced flexibility to less relapselike behavior in rats. In these experiments, rats initially learned to press a lever to receive cocaine intravenously, but they then learned to stop pressing after the lever started delivering saline instead. When given a small "reminder" dose of cocaine or a cue associated with the drug, the control rats began pressing the lever again. The rodents treated with NAC pressed the lever substantially less often than controls.

Drugs do more than interfere with glutamate pumps, however. They also change the synaptic machinery responsible for detecting glutamate–which means another possible target for treatment. There are several types of glutamate receptors, each of which shapes the ensuing electrical signal in distinctive ways. These receptors interact, meaning that drug-induced changes to one receptor can affect other receptor types, causing a kind of domino effect of molecular adjustments. "I don't think there's one monolithic thing that's broken at this synapse, but rather one thing after another is somewhat shifted," says Marina Wolf, a neuroscientist at the Rosalind Franklin University of Medicine and Science.

In 2008 Wolf and her team found that prolonged access to cocaine spurred a long-lasting increase in an unusual kind of glutamate receptor in rats that matched an uptick in the rodents' drug cravings. In 2011 they reported that pharmacologically stimulating another type of glutamate receptor reversed the effect, possibly by instigating the removal of the unusual receptors.

Recovery Fast Track

Many of the drug-induced changes in glutamate signaling can be targeted with compounds that doctors already use for other ailments. Some glutamate receptor drugs are approved for treating disorders such as migraines or Parkinson's disease, and NAC is even sold in health food stores as an antioxidant.

Preliminary studies in humans suggest that taking NAC does indeed reduce drug use. Kalivas and his colleagues reported in a series of recent studies that three days of NAC treatment decreased—but did not eliminate—cocaine users' desire for the drug, and a similar treatment regimen halved craving intensity for cocaine, as reported by frequent users. Other studies have also found that NAC treatment in adult pack-a-day smokers and teenage marijuana users reduced consumption in both groups.

Kalivas calls his results in humans "modest" compared with the strength of the rat studies, however. NAC may need more time to recondition the synapses in people, and it may work best when ongoing drug use does not interfere. To test this idea, he has begun a study in which participants will abstain from drugs while receiving NAC in the hospital for six weeks.

Even with new pharmacological remedies on the horizon, behavioral therapies that teach coping strategies to an addict will still form a crucial part of treatment. "Restoring the synaptic machinery will not do anything on its own," Kalivas says. "A person has to have other input that will help guide him or her away from the drugs." Although people can and do beat addiction solely through therapies such as 12-step programs, restoring the synapses pharmaceutically may ease the way for the plans formulated in the prefrontal cortex to hold sway over behavior.

This type of treatment could speed up recovery for people such as Reid, who tried and failed several times to get sober. After a humiliating arrest for driving under the influence, he began taking a drug that blocks the metabolism of alcohol, so that if he has a drink he becomes sick. That threat, combined with counseling and a 12-step program, has helped him stay sober since January 2011. He says it is the hardest thing he has ever done, however, and his old habits continue to haunt him. A drug that directly targets these habit-forming areas of the brain, such as NAC, might have made his recovery easier. "There will be a time today when I think a cold beer would really be nice," he says. "But I just have to get through it and move on."

Referenced

Impulsivity Resulting from Frontostriatal Dysfunction in Drug Abuse: Implications for the Control of Behavior by Reward-Related Stimuli. J. D. Jentsch and J. R. Taylor in *Psychopharmacology* (Berlin), Vol. 146, No. 4, pages 373–390; October 1999.

Reversing Cocaine-Induced Synaptic Potentiation Provides Enduring Protection from Relapse. Khaled Moussawi et al. in *Proceedings of the National Academy of Sciences USA*, Vol. 108, No. 1, pages 385–390; January 4, 2011.

New Medications for Drug Addiction Hiding in Glutamatergic Neuroplasticity. P. W. Kalivas and N. D. Volkow in *Molecular Psychiatry*, Vol. 16, No. 10, pages 974–986; October 2011.

A Double-Blind Randomized Controlled Trial of N-acetylcysteine in Cannabis-Dependent Adolescents. K. M. Gray et al. in *American Journal of Psychiatry*, Vol. 169, No. 8, pages 805–812; August 2012.

About the Author

Michele Solis is a freelance science writer and former neuroscientist who lives in Seattle.

Food, Sex, Gambling, the Internet: When Is It Addiction?

By Carl Erik Fisher

Theo did not seem like the type to become addicted to gambling. He was a literary star who had published his first novel at age 24 to great success. While traveling through Europe, he began visiting elegant casinos, at first dabbling in table games like roulette. With time, though, this pleasant diversion became a compulsion, and he lost nearly all his money in just a few years. He continued to produce critically acclaimed books—at one point churning out a new novel in less than a month to settle urgent debts—but he struggled to stay afloat, and his wife soon had to sell her jewelry. Remarkably, aside from the gambling, his life seemed fine. His writing was respected, and his family life was satisfying. He was simply hooked.

"Theo" is actually Fyodor Dostoyevsky, the prototypical gambling addict. Despite profound insight into the human condition, Dostoyevsky struggled with gambling for many years and was almost financially ruined several times. His semiautobiographical novel *The Gambler*—written to cover his debts, published in 1867—described compulsive gambling so well that 20th-century psychiatrists studied it as a model for the concept of gambling addiction.

Well over a century ago people already realized that an individual could have what is today called a behavioral addiction: an overwhelming, repetitive and harmful pattern of behaviors apart from drug or alcohol abuse. Now, 150 years after Dostoyevsky first walked into the casinos of Romantic-era Europe, addictions to sex, eating, video games and other behaviors are getting serious recognition in some quarters of medicine and among the public. Casualties of behavioral addictions are appearing in the news: not just gamblers throwing their life savings away but also porn addicts masturbating to iPhones on the freeway and even babies left to die by parents engrossed in video games. Doubters, however, argue that slapping the addiction label on these habits inappropriately excuses bad behavior.

Are these behaviors mental disorders? Many people are striving to limit their screen time or watch their diets, but does that mean that Internet and food addiction epidemics are upon us? Proponents argue, neuroscience evidence in hand, that behavioral addictions are brain disorders, but critics question those interpretations and protest that we are unnecessarily medicalizing everyday suffering.

This leaves psychiatrists like me in a difficult position. In my practice in New York City, I received more inquiries in the past year from people seeking help for Internet addiction than for cocaine and heroin addiction combined. It is hard to deny that for some of them, behavioral addictions are real–these individuals are truly overwhelmed by repetitive, harmful behaviors. Their schooling, marriage or job is in danger because of their uncontrolled actions. They sincerely want to stop, but they feel powerless. A mental disorder is defined simply as a dysfunctional thought process or behavior that causes harm. In my view, some behavioral addictions clearly meet that description–there is a reason we have had this intuition since the time of Dostoyevsky.

Yet many people rush to diagnose themselves with behavioral addictions, not recognizing the underlying depression or anxiety driving their problems. Treatment for them may have different considerations, and research is just starting to offer clues about how to help these different types of addictions. After all, that is the goal of all the questions and debates–how can we best help people who are suffering?

As I set out to understand this phenomenon, I found that even the experts within the field are divided–and that includes those who support the idea of behavioral addiction. But along the way I also caught glimpses of paths toward a resolution.

Disordered Desires

People were making unhealthy choices about sex, eating and money well before Dostoyevsky. Saint Augustine's *Confessions*, written sometime around the year 400, intricately explores loss of control over sexual impulses. The root of the word "addiction" itself is thought to come from the Latin term for "dedication," and prior to the 19th century the word was often used to describe behaviors in a positive light, such as being dedicated to public service or "addicted to books." But a darker view of addiction soon began to emerge.

In the 20th century the temperance movement, the development of psychiatry and the growth of Alcoholics Anonymous all shaped the disease model of addiction: loss of control over drugs and alcohol is a chronic, relapsing, lifelong disorder. As early as 1957, offshoot 12-step programs such as Gamblers Anonymous and Overeaters Anonymous applied the addiction model to problems that did not involve drugs or alcohol.

In 1980 "pathological gambling" was added to the *Diagnostic and Statistical Manual* (*DSM*), the American Psychiatric Association's official categorization of mental disorders, as a condition deserving further study. In 1990 Isaac Marks, a psychiatric researcher in London, penned a widely cited editorial in the *British Journal of Addiction* describing "non-chemical" addictions, and since then the idea has received increasing attention from mainstream researchers and clinicians.

In popular culture, behavioral addictions are also getting much more recognition. Movies such as *Shame* and *Don Jon* vividly portray sex and pornography addictions. For better or for worse, sex addiction is the go-to excuse for unfaithful celebrities. Residential rehabilitation centers for Internet addiction are booming in China and even starting to appear in the U.S. Additionally, as developed countries grapple with obesity, a food-addiction model is increasingly used to explain some people's uncontrolled eating.

At the same time, however, the academic understanding of addiction is a conceptual minefield. Organized psychiatry has long shied away from even using the word "addiction." The *DSM* formerly called it "dependence," a stand-in term that emphasized the idea of addiction as a chronic, relapsing disease that is markedly different from other unhealthy drug and alcohol use.

That distinction, between "true" addiction and other harmful patterns of drug abuse, has been struck from the latest edition, the *DSM-5*, published in 2013. The update radically altered the definition of addiction, collapsing both "dependence" and milder forms of "substance abuse" into one condition, "substance use disorder," with no clear division between mild and extreme cases. That decision was based on data from more than 200,000 research participants, which showed an even continuum from the worst cases down to less severe substance-use problems.

This changing understanding of addiction makes it even more difficult to know how to define behavioral addictions. Is gambling addiction like drug addiction, or is it something else? The evidence base for most behavioral addictions is far less robust than for substance addictions, but research is beginning to fill in the gaps.

Gambling Gets Its Due

Researchers have increasingly used the tools of neuroscience to argue that behavioral addictions are brain-based disorders. For example, as recently as the early 2000s clinicians were not sure how to categorize pathological gambling. Some thought it looked more like obsessive-compulsive disorder than drug or alcohol addiction. From their perspective, pumping quarters into slot machines or repetitively washing one's hands appeared almost the same—irrational, compulsive and almost automatic.

Marc N. Potenza, a gambling researcher at Yale University, published an enlightening study in 2003. Using functional MRI, a method for assessing blood flow in the brain, his team measured the cerebral activity of people with gambling problems as they watched provocative videos in the scanner: the thrill of an unexpected windfall, the clatter of new chips, the flutter of cards.

The imaging revealed decreased activity in the ventromedial prefrontal cortex (vmPFC), an area in the middle of the frontal lobes associated with regulating impulses. People with OCD show the opposite result: they have increased vmPFC activation during obsessions, indicating excessive thoughts and preoccupations. These and subsequent imaging findings show that the brain activity of problem gamblers looks similar to that of drug and alcohol addicts.

In 2005 a group of researchers in Hamburg, Germany, used fMRI to discover further similarities between behavioral and substance addictions. They measured responses in the ventral striatum, a deep-brain structure rich in dopamine and associated with sensitivity to rewards. Drug and alcohol addicts have been shown to have both reduced activity in the ventral striatum and altered dopamine levels. This lowered activity is consistent with the idea of a reward deficiency: people with addictions have blunted responses to rewards, driving them to compensate by seeking even more gratification. Sure enough, the gamblers in this study showed less activity in the ventral striatum.

Such findings supported the formal addition of "gambling disorder" to the DSM-5. The only other behavioral addiction to be added was "Internet gaming disorder," but only in the appendix as a condition for further study. Debates were fierce, however, about behavioral addictions in general, and scientific commonalities between behavioral and substance addictions were the crux of the proponents' argument.

A Lot Like Drugs

Much scientific research on behavioral addictions has focused on comparing and contrasting them with substance dependence. Aside from bolstering their status as disorders, doing so can offer clues as to whether similar treatments might work, if such interventions should be covered by insurance companies, and how society should treat people who suffer from these afflictions.

There has been a plethora of fMRI studies since Potenza's influential gambling studies. His initial findings have been replicated several times, and the brain areas implicated are relatively consistent. Preliminary brain-imaging studies have found some similar results in food, sex and Internet addiction, although the results are not always consistent. Overall the findings are not as well aligned with findings from traditional substance-use disorder research.

Investigation of the neurochemistry of these disorders is also preliminary, but some researchers have found altered neurotransmitter receptor function in people with food and Internet addictions. Studies using positron-emission tomography have shown, for example, lower levels of activity in dopamine-producing regions of the ventral striatum at rest in both obese people and people with Internet addiction. PET studies of compulsive gamblers, however, have shown conflicting results. In food addiction, a growing body of evidence from rodents shows changes in neurotransmitters such as dopamine. So although there are interesting clues from neurochemistry, the jury is still out.

Another clue that behavioral addiction may be quite similar to substance addiction is the fact that some pharmaceutical treatments appear to work for both conditions. For example, naltrexone, a drug that blocks opioid receptors in the brain, has successfully treated alcohol and opioid dependence since the 1990s. More recent evidence shows that it can help with gambling addiction, and some smaller trials hint that it might ease sex addiction.

These confluences suggest that behavioral and substance addictions might have the same underlying causes–as does the fact that large population surveys show that the two types of addiction tend to occur together. Such findings are often comforting to people who wonder why they cannot overcome a repetitive behavior–framing it as a "real" addiction can mitigate shame and speed recovery. For me and other clinicians, the similarities between behavioral addictions and drug addictions help us choose and be confident in our therapeutic strategies.

Yet just as with substance addicts, people who show signs of behavioral problems often have other mental disorders that may be complicating the diagnostic picture. To give them the best treatment, sometimes it is important to look more closely at what underlies their behaviors.

Why Me?

Patients with behavioral addictions often ask me whether they are fated to be addicts—whether their battles for control are an intrinsic part of their character. We have known for many years that genetic factors explain up to 50 percent of the risk for developing addictions, including problem gambling. Just recently, genetic studies of other behavioral addictions have found similar results. A 2014 study of more than 800 Chinese twins and a 2015 study of more than 5,000 Dutch twins both found that, statistically, genetic factors explained approximately half the risk of compulsive Internet use. The exact genetic contributions, however, are too complicated to make interpretations based on an individual's genetic makeup.

Other factors can be set in motion before a person's birth, as illustrated by rodent research of food addiction. In one 2010 study, mouse mothers on a high-calorie, high-fat diet transmitted an exaggerated preference for fat to their offspring, as compared with control mice on a normal diet. This preference appeared to be passed down through epigenetic alterations that effect the expression of the genes responsible for dopamine-managing proteins in the brain.

Life experience, early exposure and a host of other environmental factors probably play a role in steering a person toward an addiction—the reality is that only a small percentage of people who engage with potentially addictive substances or behaviors end up hooked, and scientists know very little about why. Unfortunately, brain-imaging studies cannot answer that question. If you could go back in time and put Dostoyevsky in a scanner, he would almost definitely show altered activation in his brain's reward centers, but that would not necessarily tell you that gambling was his fundamental problem.

Maybe he was instead driven by existential angst, or the trauma of his Siberian exile, or even his documented case of temporal lobe epilepsy.

Explaining the mechanism is not the same as revealing the cause. From the fMRI studies of brain activation down to the intricate functions of neurotransmitters, the issue of causality is a big sticking point for the interpretation of this research. The basics are clear: the brain has circuits that respond to the feeling of pleasure and the anticipation of reward. In some vulnerable individuals, these circuits adapt in response to extreme repetitions of pleasurable activities. Yet this process speaks only to *how*, not *why*; what ultimately drives the behavior remains unexplained.

An unexpected illustration of this mystery comes from the treatment of Parkinson's disease. The illness is treated with drugs that act directly on dopamine receptors, and because the drugs disrupt the reward system, some people with Parkinson's develop compulsive behaviors. For some, eating, sex or gambling becomes addictive. Others abuse the drugs themselves, taking more than prescribed and doctor shopping for extra doses. But plenty of people do not develop any compulsive behaviors, even though they experience the same underlying influence–an introduction of powerful dopamine-acting drugs.

Reducing the anatomy of addiction to the "reward system," therefore, is too simple. Yet discussions of the reward system dominate the scientific discourse about addictions, in part because it is challenging to integrate all the other dimensions that matter–social, psychological, even philosophical concerns.

Societal Costs

When hypersexual disorder was proposed as a new diagnosis, critics in the psychiatric community expressed concern about the social and legal ramifications. Would the disorder be misused in court cases involving sex offenders? Would residential treatment centers pop up to unfairly profit from fad diagnoses, or would the disorder be used as an excuse for sexual predation?

Beyond the concrete risks, there is a popular notion that medicalizing behaviors such as compulsive sex and shopping might cast people in an undeserved sick role. There is some value, the argument goes, in preserving the opprobrium that society usually levels at philanderers and spendthrifts. Negative public perception might actually help keep some people in check, whereas a new diagnosis might inappropriately absolve them of responsibility.

If more behavioral addictions are classified as mental disorders—as they almost surely will be, with proponents continuing to muster neuroscientific evidence—there will be societal consequences. Insurance coverage, disability determinations, or the public's understanding of "mad versus bad"—the stakes are high. On the other hand, restricting the recognition of behavioral addictions could curtail identification of and treatment for people who are truly in pain. As long as a behavioral addiction is causing significant harm in a person's life, I believe it needs to be recognized.

This issue of harm, however, is sometimes missed by researchers, which leads to some odd proposals. For example, French researchers recently suggested "tango addiction." They claimed to have found that one third of recreational dancers had symptoms of craving and that 20 percent had physical withdrawal symptoms related to the (admittedly captivating) Argentine dance. The problem, as even those researchers admit, is they could not find any good evidence of tango causing real problems in people's lives.

The gray area between clear disorders and unhealthy habits is rightfully controversial. Sometimes when people ask if they should call themselves addicts, I have to reply that I don't know. We are in the midst of clarifying and even redefining what addiction means, with our eye constantly on the end goal—to help the people who are suffering from these plights.

The Way Forward

A paradigm shift is happening in psychiatry, and many researchers now say that *no* mental illness fits into a neat diagnostic category. In fact, the National Institute of Mental Health is completely revamping its research program to focus less on lumping together symptoms and more on exploring the specific genetic and neurobiological elements of mental disorders. In this way, behavioral addictions are a case study in one of the trickiest problems in psychiatry: how to characterize disorders that have no definitive brain scan, no blood test and no gold standard. With time, and with more research into the underlying causes of such behaviors, we may be better able to help those who feel helpless and out of control.

One promising area of research suggests that any given type of behavioral addiction–say, Internet gaming disorder–might not be one neat disorder but rather an assortment of different underlying problems that happen to manifest the same way. This idea of subtypes was first articulated in 2000 by Alex Blaszczynski, a psychology professor who studies gambling at the University of Sydney. He and his colleague Lia Nower, a professor of social work at Rutgers University, proposed three subgroups of gambling addiction: behaviorally conditioned gamblers who get in the habit of chasing wins and losses, emotionally vulnerable gamblers who are responding to anxiety or depression, and antisocial gamblers who are dysfunctionally impulsive across the board.

Nower and Blaszczynski recently studied data from more than 500 problem gamblers, drawn from an addiction study of more than 43,000 people, and found three distinct groups that matched their model: one group with milder symptoms, one with more co-occurring psychiatric disorders, and one with severe impulsivity across many areas of life. Also, in studies of online gaming, investigators have found distinct motivations similar to Blaszczynski and Nower's model: a preoccupation with mastery (behavioral conditioning), a compensation for real-life problems, or a response to social anxiety (reactions to emotional problems). Although the evidence is still pending, some researchers believe the subgroup model can also be applied to hypersexual behavior.

The point of all these diagnostic refinements, of course, is to help the sufferers of addiction. Unfortunately, studies of treatments tailored to those subtypes have not yet shown any added benefit. Indeed, researchers in the field of substance-use disorder have argued over possible "typologies" of drug and alcohol addiction for decades, and there is still no clear consensus emerging. Perhaps the current models, which are based only on outwardly observable features of addictions, are incomplete. Diagnosis may have to go beyond the psychological features of addicts and look at their underlying genetics and neurochemistry. For example, in the substance-addiction field, researchers have recently shown that variations in genes for specific neurotransmitter receptors can predict addicts' responses to medications such as naltrexone. Considering how new this work is, the behavioral-addiction field may need time to catch up.

In the meantime, a flexible and holistic approach to treatment is best. People who consider themselves Internet addicts or sex addicts, whose problems are complicated by social anxiety or depression or other issues, need more attention to the emotional component of their behavior, as opposed to those who fit the traditional model of addiction and feel stuck in an automatic cycle of stimulus and response. Research has shown that when people have both substance-use problems and other emotional issues, we get the best results by treating all issues simultaneously.

My own approach is to aim for this inclusive mind-set. We have to assume we do not have all the answers. People cannot simply be reduced to their "hijacked" reward systems, and there is no single, unassailably correct diagnosis of or treatment for addiction. Someday a new wave of research findings may help make finer distinctions more precisely. For now, though, we do the best we can by trying to learn as much about our patients as possible.

There are no easy answers. As the examples of Dostoyevsky and Saint Augustine show us, we humans have been endeavoring for ages to understand why we get stuck in patterns of harmful behaviors and why for some the consequences from losing control are truly severe. As we begin to focus on this problem with real scientific rigor, the right question might not be "Is this real?" but rather "How can we help?"

Referenced

Do We All Have Behavioral Addictions? Allen Frances in *Huffington Post*; March 28, 2012.

A Targeted Review of the Neurobiology and Genetics of Behavioural Addictions: An Emerging Area of Research. Robert F. Leeman and Marc N. Potenza in *Canadian Journal of Psychiatry/ Revue Canadienne de Psychiatrie*, Vol. 58, No. 5, pages 260–273; May 2013.

Controversies about Hypersexual Disorder and the DSM-5. Rory C. Reid and Martin P. Kafka in *Current Sexual Health Reports*, Vol. 6, No. 4, pages 259–264; December 2014.

Disordered Gambling: The Evolving Concept of Behavioral Addiction. Luke Clark in *Annals of the New York Academy of Sciences*, Vol. 1327, pages 46–61; 2014.

Are We Overpathologizing Everyday Life? A Tenable Blueprint for Behavioral Addiction Research. Joel Billieux, Adriano Schimmenti, Yasser Khazaal, Pierre Maurage and Alexandre Heeren in *Journal of Behavioral Addictions*, Vol. 4, No. 3, pages 119–123. Published online May 27, 2015.

About the Author

Carl Erik Fisher is assistant professor of clinical psychiatry at Columbia University. He works in the Division of Law, Ethics, and Psychiatry and teaches in the university's Masters in Bioethics program.

Electrical Brain Stimulation May Alleviate Obsessive-Compulsive Behaviors

By Diana Kwon

Obsessive-compulsive disorder (OCD) is marked by repetitive, anxiety-inducing thoughts, urges and compulsions, such as excessive cleaning, counting and checking. These behaviors are also prevalent in the general population: one study in a large sample of U.S. adults found more than a quarter had experienced obsessions or compulsions at some point in their life. Although most of these individuals do not develop full-blown OCD, such symptoms can still interfere with daily life. A new study, published on January 18 in *Nature Medicine*, hints that these behaviors may be alleviated by stimulating the brain with an electrical current—without the need to insert electrodes under the skull.

Robert Reinhart, a neuroscientist at Boston University, and his group drew on two parallel lines of research for this study. First, evidence suggests that obsessive-compulsive behaviors may arise as a result of overlearning habits—leading to their excessive repetition—and abnormalities in brain circuits involved in learning from rewards. Separately, studies point to the importance of high-frequency rhythms in the so-called high-beta/low-gamma range (also referred to as simply beta-gamma) in decision-making and learning from positive feedback.

Drawing on these prior observations, Shrey Grover, a doctoral student in Reinhart's lab, hypothesized with others in the team that manipulating beta-gamma rhythms in the orbitofrontal cortex (OFC)—a key region in the reward network located in the front of the brain—might disrupt the ability to repetitively pursue rewarding choices. In doing so, the researchers thought, the intervention could reduce obsessive-compulsive behaviors associated with maladaptive habits.

To test this hypothesis, Grover and his colleagues carried out a two-part study. The first segment was aimed at identifying whether the high-frequency brain activity influenced how well people were able to learn from rewards. The team recruited 60 volunteers and first used electroencephalography to pinpoint the unique frequencies of beta-gamma rhythms in the OFC that were active in a given individual while that person took part in a task that involved associating symbols with monetary wins or losses. Previous work had shown that applying stimulation based on the particular patterns of rhythms in a person's brain may enhance the effectiveness of the procedure.

The participants were then split into three groups, all of whom received a noninvasive form of brain stimulation known as transcranial alternating current stimulation (tACS), which was applied to the OFC for 30 minutes over five consecutive days. Each group had a different type of stimulation: One received personalized currents tuned to an individual's beta-gamma frequencies. Another was exposed to an "active" placebo, consisting of stimulations at a lower frequency. And the third was a "passive" placebo group in which no significant current was applied to the brain. Those who received the personalized beta-gamma stimulation became less able to make optimal choices on the reward-based learning tasks–changes not observed in the two placebo groups.

Further assessment of the participants' behavior using computational models of reward-based learning suggested that the personalized tACS disrupted the learning process by making people more likely to try out different options rather than sticking with only one–even if they were less likely to result in a reward.

These findings set the stage for the second part of the study, in which the team set out to examine whether manipulating the beta-gamma rhythms typically engaged during reward-based learning would influence obsessive-compulsive behaviors. The researchers carried out a similar set of experiments on another set of volunteers: 64 people who did not have a formal OCD diagnosis but who exhibited symptoms such as checking, hoarding and obsessing.

Participants received either personalized beta-gamma stimulation or an active placebo. Those in the personalized beta-gamma group experienced a reduction in compulsive behaviors that persisted for up to three months. And those with more of those obsessive-compulsive characteristics prior to stimulation exhibited the biggest changes.

According to Grover, the team decided to study people with symptoms of OCD but no diagnosis of the disorder because researchers have increasingly been viewing obsessive-compulsive behaviors on a mild-to-severe spectrum. And even in the absence of clinically diagnosed OCD, such symptoms can cause significant distress. "By examining a nonclinical population exhibiting a range of obsessive-compulsive behaviors, we were able to examine the effectiveness of [an intervention] that may be helpful to a larger pool of individuals," Grover says. Yet the researchers' findings also suggest "that if we were to extend such an intervention to individuals diagnosed with obsessive-compulsive disorder or to other conditions of compulsivity–gambling disorder, addiction, some forms of eating disorders—we might be able to observe strong effects."

The long-lasting effects on obsessive-compulsive behaviors is "quite impressive," says Trevor Robbins, a professor of cognitive neuroscience at the University of Cambridge, who was not involved in this research. "[Neuromodulation] is certainly a treatment that should be investigated rigorously for conditions like OCD."

Carolyn Rodriguez, a psychiatrist and neuroscientist at Stanford University, who was also not involved in the study, says that because it was carried out in a nonclinical population without a formal diagnosis, the implications of these findings remain to be seen. "The neurobiology of people who are nonclinical but have these kinds of behaviors may be different than individuals who are diagnosed with OCD," she adds. "These findings are an interesting start, [but] we need to understand how it's relevant to people who have OCD." Rodriguez also points out that there are already several treatments available for the condition, including medication, therapy and a Food and Drug Administration–approved device that utilizes transcranial magnetic stimulation (TMS), a noninvasive method that uses magnetic fields to stimulate the brain. (Rodriguez is currently leading a clinical trial of TMS for OCD.)

The potential therapeutic effects of tACS on memory, food craving and other neural processes have been tested in dozens of studies in the past. Questions have been raised about whether this method actually exerts any meaningful changes in the brain, however. In the new study, what, exactly, the high-frequency tACS did to the brain remains unknown. But Grover notes that the researchers' two placebo conditions–particularly the one that involves stimulating at a different frequency–provide strong evidence that the high-frequency stimulation was responsible for the behavioral effects the team observed.

Grover and his colleagues are currently working on further experiments to pinpoint the mechanisms underlying their intervention. And they hope to conduct studies with clinical populations diagnosed with OCD in the near future. "[The recent paper] is just a preliminary step toward further understanding why this high-frequency activity is so important for obsessive-compulsive behavior," Grover says. "The fact that we can observe changes in these symptoms even now suggests there may actually be clinical benefit to this–and gives us all the more reason to try to extend the findings of this research."

About the Author

Diana Kwon is a freelance journalist who covers health and the life sciences. She is based in Berlin.

Can Obsessive-Compulsive Disorder Be Blocked in the Brain?

By Ann Graybiel and Kyle Smith

For children and adults who have conditions such as obsessive-compulsive disorder (OCD), Tourette syndrome or autism, repetitive thoughts and actions can occur even if the individuals do not want them to. In OCD a thought that repeats again and again—"my hands are dirty, my hands are dirty"—can recur in a habitual way. Such conditions occur in people from different countries and cultures, suggesting that they represent a core dysfunction related to an imbalance between behaviors. These problems appear to reflect disturbances in brain circuits that are different from, but allied with, the normal habit circuits.

Researchers in our group and that of Susanne Ahmari at the University of Pittsburgh have tested whether these OCD circuits can be controlled. Our lab group stimulated the neocortex and striatum in mice that were genetically engineered to have OCD-like traits. These mice groom themselves excessively, especially around the face. In the lab we mimicked a problem that people with OCD often have because they react excessively and repetitively to some trigger stimulus in the environment. We conditioned the mice to learn that after a tone sounded a drop of water would fall on their noses about a second later. We also performed the same routine with normal ("control") mice. The OCD-like mice started by just grooming when the water drop came, but then began to start grooming in response to the tone alone, and kept grooming all the way through when the drop fell. The control mice learned to suppress this early grooming, which after all was a wasted effort because the water drop came later. The OCD-like mice groomed compulsively every time the external cue sounded.

Using optogenetics—a technique that controls the activity of brain cells by shining light on them—we then excited a pathway that connects a small region in the cortex with the striatum. The pathway has been implicated in suppressing behaviors. This treatment immediately blocked the compulsive early grooming in the mutant mice! Yet when the water drop came, they could groom normally. And the optogenetic stimulation did not affect other normal behaviors such as eating; it selectively blocked the compulsive aspect of behavior.

These results provide tantalizing evidence that compulsive behaviors depend on pathways interconnecting the neocortex and striatum, just as entrenched habits do. Moreover, Ahmari's group has found that stimulation of a nearby part of the neocortex can actually induce repetitive behaviors that resemble those in OCD. These studies suggest that in the future therapies may be developed that could help people with such disorders.

About the Authors

Ann Graybiel is an institute professor at the Massachusetts Institute of Technology and an investigator at the McGovern Institute for Brain Research at M.I.T.

Kyle Smith is an assistant professor of psychological and brain sciences at Dartmouth College. The M.I.T. portion of the research described here was conducted by Eric Burguière.

Not-So-Quick Fix: ADHD Behavioral Therapy May Be More Effective Than Drugs in Long Run

By SciCurious

Before stimulant drugs such as Ritalin, Concerta and Adderall began their rise to popularity in the 1970s, treatment for attention-deficit hyperactivity disorder (ADHD) focused on behavioral therapy. But as concerns build over the mounting dosages and extended treatment periods that come with stimulant drugs, clinical researchers are revisiting behavioral therapy techniques. Whereas stimulant medications may help young patients focus and behave in the classroom, research now suggests that behaviorally based changes make more of a difference in the long-term.

A new synthesis of behavioral, cognitive and pharmacological findings emerged at the recent Experimental Biology meeting, held last month in San Diego, where experts in ADHD research and treatment gathered to present their work. Their findings suggest that behavioral and cognitive therapies focused on reducing impulsivity and reinforcing positive long-term habits may be able to replace current high doses of stimulant treatment in children and young adults.

Recent surveys indicate that 9 percent of all children in the U.S. have been diagnosed with ADHD. The condition's core symptoms include hyperactivity, inattention, inability to perform monotonous tasks and lack of impulse control. Children with ADHD have trouble in school and forming relationships, and 60 percent will continue to suffer from the disorder well into adulthood.

As of 2007, 2.7 million U.S. children and adolescents with ADHD were being treated with stimulant drugs. But new research reveals that these drugs are not necessarily the panacea they have been thought to be. Psychologist Claire Advokat of Louisiana State University has been looking at the effects of stimulant medications in college students to see what improves with medication and what does not. As expected, she found that people diagnosed with ADHD had lower grades and ACT (American College Testing) scores; they also dropped more classes than their peers. But she also found that these issues were not improved by stimulant medication treatment. Instead, Advokat's new findings indicate that the ADHD students naturally divided into those who had good study habits and those who did not, regardless of treatment. If students had good study habits, they did not need the medication to bolster their grades. It is not that medication has no effect; Advokat hypothesizes that "it may be that the medications can help, not in helping you remember, but in helping you form the good study habits" necessary for academic improvement. This outcome suggests that if ADHD patients could learn good study habits early on, medication could become less necessary.

Other research has examined the role of behavioral interventions not only for school-age children, but also for their parents. Parents of children with ADHD tend to exhibit more parenting-related stress and difficulties than do those of non-afflicted offspring. After training parents in stress management and giving them behavioral tools to help their children, psychologist Bill Pelham of Florida International University and his colleagues saw significant improvement in their children's ADHD-related behavior, such as the frequency of classroom disturbances.

Independently, Pelham has also shown that behavioral therapy for children also produced effects that were equal to some doses of medication. His data suggests that lower dosages combined with behavioral therapy may provide a far better outcome than stimulant medication or behavioral therapies alone.

Cognitive therapies may also boost improvement: In a 2011 PLoS ONE paper, Julie Schweitzer and colleagues in the psychiatry and behavioral sciences department and the MIND Institute at the University of California, Davis, showed that children with ADHD show extra activity in brain areas associated with "task-irrelevant" information during working memory tasks (those that depend on one's ability to hold and focus on information for immediate reasoning and recall), suggesting that they have less efficient cognitive control. New unpublished results from Schweitzer's team have shown that cognitive therapy could improve control, again potentially reducing the need for medication to "drown out" extraneous information.

Advokat, Schweitzer, Pelham and other scientists at this year's confab agreed that behavioral therapies deserve their renewed focus. These therapies create no drug-tolerance and come with no concerns about future substance abuse. The trick will be identifying which of the new therapies is most effective, and making those therapies affordable. For now, stimulant medications are much cheaper and act faster than behavioral therapy, even if the latter may be the most effective in the long run. But experts as well as parents know that the long run is what matters most.

What Internet Habits Say About Mental Health

By Adrian F. Ward and Fiercarlo Valdesolo

Consider two questions. First: Who are you? What makes you different from your peers, in terms of the things you buy, the clothes you wear, and the car you drive (or refuse to)? What makes you unique in terms of your basic psychological make-up—the part of you that makes you do the things you do, say the things you say, and feel the things you feel? And the second question: How do you use the internet?

Although these questions may seem unrelated, they're not. Clearly the *content* of your internet usage can suggest certain psychological characteristics. Spending a lot of late nights playing high stakes internet poker? Chances are you are a risk taker. Like to post videos of yourself doing karaoke on YouTube? Clearly an extravert. But what about the mechanics of your internet usage—how often you email others, chat online, stream media, or multi-task (switch from one application or website to another)? Can these behaviors—regardless of their content—also predict psychological characteristics? Recent research conducted by a team of computer scientists, engineers, and psychologists suggests that it might. Indeed, their data show that such analysis could predict a particularly important aspect of the self: the tendency to experience depression.

First, the research team asked over 200 volunteers to fill out a survey about "recent affective experiences;" what the volunteers didn't know was that a well-known measure of depression—the Center for Epidemiological Studies Depression (CES-D) scale—was embedded within this survey. The researchers then correlated scores on the hidden depression scale with individual trends in internet usage, grouped into three categories: "aggregate," which indicated how much information was being sent and received over a network, "application," which indicated the broad category of program that was being used (e.g., email, surfing the web, downloading media), and "entropy," which indicated the degree of randomness in information flow (essentially, the extent to which someone was sending and receiving information to multiple net-based resources at once).

Again, researchers didn't know *what* people were looking at on the internet (for example, depression support groups–a dead giveaway), but merely *how* they were using the internet. None of the data categories gave specific information about what websites people were visiting, the content of their emails or chats, or the types of files being downloaded–they simply indicated the extent to which people used different broad categories of net-based resources, as well as differences in people's tendency to use many resources at once.

It turns out that very specific patterns of internet use are reliably related to depressive tendencies. For example, peer-to-peer file sharing, heavy emailing and chatting online, and a tendency to quickly switch between multiple websites and other online resources all predict a greater propensity to experience symptoms of depression. Although the exact reasons that these behaviors predict depression is unknown, each behavior corresponds with previous research on depression. Quickly switching between websites may reflect anhedonia (a decreased ability to experience emotions), as people desperately seek for emotional stimulation. Similarly, excessive emailing and chatting may signify a relative lack of strong face-to-face relationships, as people strive to maintain contact either with faraway friends or new people met online.

These data are particularly important for several reasons. Depression is both prevalent and dangerous. Recent estimates from the Centers for Disease Control and Prevention (CDC) indicate that around 10 percent of adults in the United States currently suffer from clinical depression–depression that consists of symptoms such as disruptions in eating, sleeping, and concentration patterns, lack of interest in daily activities, and consistently feeling like a failure. These estimates are even higher for other segments of the population; for example, a 2011 report by the American College Health Association found that 30 percent of college students have "felt so depressed that it was difficult to function" within the past year.

Despite the serious negative consequences of living with depression, the condition is notoriously hard to diagnose. Estimates suggest that as many as two thirds of people living with depression do not realize that they have a treatable condition and, as a result, do not seek treatment. Even those who do seek treatment–either voluntarily or at the request of friends, family members, or doctors–are often ashamed to admit to their symptoms. Any diagnosis relying on self-report–whether it be a self-administered test or a clinical interview in a doctor's office–is prone to selective reporting. No one wants to be depressed and, as a result, many people suffering from depression may answer from the perspective of how they *want* to feel, rather than how they *actually* feel.

In this way, diagnosing people at risk for depression is similar to diagnosing people at risk for committing suicide. Those most vulnerable –the people who actually intend to carry out the act–are unlikely to reveal this information. As a result, clinical psychologists have developed ways to test for suicidal intentions that circumvent self-report issues; for example, by using implicit methods that may reveal intentions of which the patients themselves are unaware.

Perhaps the most exciting implication of the data linking internet usage to depression is the possibility that clues of depressive tendencies can also be identified early, not only before the opportunity for professional diagnosis but perhaps also before people are aware of it themselves. An intervention as simple as tracking internet use may allow depression, a prevalent and dangerous illness, to be discovered and treated earlier, more effectively, and for more people.

About the Authors

Adrian F. Ward is a doctoral candidate in the Department of Psychology at Harvard University. His doctoral research is focused on the relationships between technology, cognition, social relationships, and self-esteem.

Piercarlo Valdesolo is an Assistant Professor of Psychology at Claremont McKenna College, and co-author of the book Out of Character.

GLOSSARY

afflict To cause pain or suffering.

aspiration Something a person wants very much to achieve.

aversion A feeling of not liking something.

cognition The ability to think and understand.

compulsion A strong desire to do something.

constraint Something that limits something or someone.

dorsomedial prefrontal cortex The section of the brain that plays a role in a person's sense of self and decision-making.

drudgery Boring and difficult work.

elation The feeling of being happy and/or excited.

eudaemonia A feeling of happiness or well-being as defined by the Greek philosopher Aristotle.

filibuster An effort to delay.

fortitude Mental strength or courage.

gratifying The feeling of being happy or satisfied.

ingrained Existing for a long time and difficult to be changed.

intervention The act of interfering or affecting the outcome of something.

minutiae Small details.

neuroscience The scientific study of the nerves, learning, and behavior.

obsessive-compulsive disorder An anxiety condition marked by obsessions or compulsions that interfere with daily functioning.

optimal Best or most effective.

trivial Unimportant.

FURTHER INFORMATION

Balleine, Bernard W. and John P. O'Doherty. "Human and Rodent Homologies in Action Control: Corticostriatal Determinants of Goal-Directed and Habitual Action," *Neuropsychopharmacology*, 2010, https://www.nature.com/articles/npp2009131.

Burguière, Eric et al. "Optogenetic Stimulation of Lateral Orbitofronto-Striatal Pathway Suppresses Compulsive Behaviors," *Science*, June 7, 2013, https://www.science.org/doi/10.1126/science.1232380.

Clark, Luke. "Disordered Gambling: The Evolving Concept of Behavioral Addiction," *Annals of the New York Academy of Sciences*, 2014, https://nyaspubs.onlinelibrary.wiley.com/doi/10.1111/nyas.12558.

Graybiel, Ann M. "Habits, Rituals, and the Evaluative Brain," *Annual Review of Neuroscience*, July 2008, https://www.annualreviews.org/doi/abs/10.1146/annurev.neuro.29.051605.112851.

Leeman, Robert F. and Marc N. Potenza. "A Targeted Review of the Neurobiology and Genetics of Behavioural Addictions: An Emerging Area of Research," *Canadian Journal of Psychiatry*, May 2013, https://journals.sagepub.com/doi/10.1177/070674371305800503.

Sirois, Fuschia and Timothy Pychyl. "Procrastination and the Priority of Short-Term Mood Regulation: Consequences for Future Self," *Social and Personality Psychology Compass*, February 2013,, https://compass.onlinelibrary.wiley.com/doi/10.1111/spc3.12011.

Steel, Piers. "The Nature of Procrastination: A Meta-Analytic and Theoretical Review of Quintessential Self-Regulatory Failure," *Psychological Bulletin*, 2007, https://psycnet.apa.org/doiLanding?doi=10.1037%2F0033-2909.133.1.65.

CITATIONS

1.1 How the Brain Makes and Breaks Habits by Anne M. Graybiel and Kyle S. Smith (June 1, 2014); 1.2 Using Behavioral Science to Build an Exercise Habit by Katherine L. Milkman and Angela Duckworth (May 1, 2018); 1.3 Nail Biting May Arise from Perfectionism by Susan Cosier (July 1, 2015); 1.4 When Old Habits Die Easy by Christie Nicholson (November 25, 2012); 1.5 Tracking Your Steps and Other Behaviors Isn't Always the Greatest Idea by Zeynep Tufekci (May 1, 2019); 1.6 Self-Tracking Your 2020 Resolutions by Enrique Rueda and Karla Erickson (January 2, 2020); 2.1 New Year's Resolutions are Notoriously Slippery, but Science Can Help You Keep Them by Katy Milkman (January 11, 2022); 2.2 The Best New Year's Resolution Might Be to Just Let Go of an Unfulfilled Life Goal by Francine Russo (December 28, 2022); 2.3 Why We Think We Can Keep Those New Year's Resolutions by Benjamin A. Converse and Marie Hennecke (December 29, 2016); 2.4 How Would a Psychologist Get in Shape? by Victoria Stern (January 1, 2015); 2.5 How to Stick to Your New Year Resolutions by Susana Martinez-Conde (January 1, 2016); 2.6 How to Be an Optimal Human by Scott Barry Kaufman (February 7, 2016); 3.1 Procrastinating Again? How to Kick the Habit by Trisha Gura (December 1, 2008); 3.2 Pre-Crastination: The Opposite of Procrastination by David A. Rosenbaum and Edward A. Wasserman (June 30, 2015); 3.3 Sloth: To Stop Procrastinating, Focus on Emotions by Sandra Upson (November 1, 2013); 3.4 'Cognitive Prosthesis' Enhances Productivity by Diana Kwon (November 1, 2019); 3.5 Why Do Today What You Can Put Off Until Tomorrow by David Biello (January 15, 2007); 3.6 Training the Brain's Motivation Center by Matthew A. Scult (April 25, 2016); 3.7 Pinpointing the Brain's Motivation Switch by Leslie Nemo (July 13, 2017); 4.1 Why Feeling Close to the Finish Line Makes You Push Harder by Katy Milkman and Kassie Brabaw (June 9, 2020); 4.2 Having a 'Plan B' Can Hurt Your Chances of Success by Katherine Milkman and Jihae Shin (July 19, 2016); 4.3 Need More Self-Control? Try a Simple Ritual by Francesca Gino (August 21, 2018); 4.4 A Self-Improvement Secret: Work on Strengths by Lauren Howe (May 24, 2016); 4.5 How to Avoid the Temptations of Immediate Gratification by Melanie Bauer (January 15, 2013); 5.1 Disrupting the Habits of Anorexia by Deborah R. Glasofer and Joanna Steinglass (September 1, 2016); 5.2 Enhancing the Brain's Flexibility Could Unseat Addiction by Michele Solis (March 1, 2013); 5.3 Food, Sex, Gambling, the Internet: When Is It Addiction? by Carl Erik Fisher (January 1, 2016); 5.4 Electrical Brain Stimulation May Alleviate Obsessive-Compulsive Behaviors by Diana Kwon (January 19, 2021); 5.5 Can Obsessive-Compulsive Disorder Be Blocked in the Brain? by Ann Graybiel and Kyle Smith (June 1, 2014); 5.6 Not-So-Quick Fix: ADHD Behavioral Therapy May Be More Effective Than Drugs in Long Run by SciCurious (May 15, 2012); 5.7 What Internet Habits Say About Mental Health by Adrian F. Ward and Fiercarlo Valdesolo (August 14, 2012).

Each author biography was accurate at the time the article was originally published.

INDEX

R

S